Hearty & Healthy
D*a*IRY COOKBOOK

Executive Editor	Nick Rowe
Managing Editor	Emily Anderson
Editor	Emma Callery
Designer	Karen Perry
Picture Researcher	Emma Thackara
Food Illustrations	Bob Hook
Proof Reader	Aune Butt
Indexer	Hilary Bird
Photographers	Steve Lee
	Tony Briscoe
Food Stylist	Sara Lewis
Props Stylist	Jo Harris
Recipes created by	Pat Alburey
	Kathryn Hawkins
	Sue McMahon
	Kate Moseley
Nutritional Consultant	Dr Wendy Doyle
Recipe testers	Angela Broad
	Sarah Broad
	Helen Cookson
	Art Devlin
	Carolyn Glazebrook
	Katy Johnson
	Melanie Meadowcroft
	Sandra Meadowcroft
	Claire Nadin
	Chris Perry
	Peter Tantram
Production	Priti Kothary
	Teresa Wellborne

Eaglemoss Consumer Publications Ltd
Electra House, Electra Way, Crewe, Cheshire, CW1 6WZ
Telephone 01270 270050 Website www.dairydiary.co.uk

First printed March 2007
© Eaglemoss Consumer Publications Ltd
ISBN-13: 978-0-9554232-1-5
1 2 3 4 5 6 7 8 9

Contents

The health facts

This introduction explains WHY we should all eat healthily, WHAT that really means in terms of the range of foods we eat, and HOW we can improve our diet and avoid the 'nasties' that seem such a good idea at the time but, in fact, do so much damage to our bodies. This may help you make a few decisions about diet and lifestyle that really could change your life.

Despite the hustle and bustle of today's busy lifestyle we often consume far more food than we really need. This excess consumption of energy results in fat building up in our bodies with consequent health problems in later life. But we can do something about it and the vital first step is to eat healthily.

This book will help you and your family to eat healthily and heartily by following simple rules about what you eat and how you cook it. Faddy diets and obsessive calorie counting can take the joy out of eating, and it is well documented that much of weight lost through special diets returns pretty quickly. You'll see (and taste!) that these recipes help you to eat well, keep well and enjoy good food.

Eating healthily

A healthy diet is a balanced diet that includes foods from the five food groups (see below). It should be low in fat but need not be low in flavours or interest. The key to feeding yourself and your family is to understand what is in different foods, how and why we should eat them and in roughly what quantities.

Carbohydrates Many people fear carbohydrates will make them fat. In reality, it is what we add to them that has the fat – such as the butter or margarine that contains twice as many

The famous five

Food group	Found in	Contains	Daily quantity
Starchy carbohydrates	Bread, cereals, pasta, potatoes, rice	Carbohydrates, energy, fibre, minerals, protein, vitamins	About a third of your calories: 6–11 servings
Fruits and vegetables	All such foods, whether they are fresh, canned, frozen or dried	Fibre, minerals, vitamins and phytochemicals	5 servings
Protein	Beans and pulses, eggs, lean red and white meat, fish, nuts and seeds	Iron, protein	2–4 servings
Dairy	Cheese, milk, yogurt	Calcium, fat, protein, vitamins	2–3 low-fat servings
Fats and sugars	Biscuits, butter, cakes, cream	Fatty acids	Moderate quantities

calories as the slice of bread it covers, or the rich creamy sauce that is served with a bowl of pasta. Ideally, the less processed the food, the better; the bread should be wholemeal (white bread loses most of its nutrients during processing), and the rice should be brown for the same reason.

Fruits and vegetables The deeper the colour of foods in this group, the more nutritious they are. Cover all bases by going for a 'rainbow' approach so you eat across the range. Potatoes, sweet potatoes and yams are not classified as vegetables – they fall into the carbohydrates group. As well as vitamins and minerals, fruit and vegetables are also a source of phytochemicals (also known as phytonutrients), substances that promote the immune system and help the body fight a variety of diseases.

Dairy Foods such as milk, yogurt and cheese are a major source of calcium, which strengthens teeth and bones. Reduced-fat variants, such as skimmed milk, contain a similar amount of this essential mineral, but young children should have full-fat versions. Dairy products also contain other minerals, such as phosphorus and magnesium.

Protein Buy meat that is as lean as possible, with fat cut off before cooking or drained off during it. About half of the fish you eat should be oil-rich varieties such as salmon, mackerel or tuna. It is perfectly possible to obtain all the protein we need from the vegetarian options in this group.

Fats and sugars This group includes many of the foods we (and especially children) really enjoy eating. This is partly because sweet foods, such as chocolate, release brain-pleasing endorphins so that shortly after you eat them, you want more. Sugar is full of calories, with no nutritional benefit at all.

What's a serving?

A serving of ...	is obtained through ...
Fruit	• One medium item, such as an apple or banana, or two small fruits, such as an apricot • A handful of berries or 75g (3oz) chopped, cooked or canned fruit • 45g (1½oz) dried fruit • 175ml (6fl oz) fruit juice
Vegetables	• 50g (2oz) of raw, leafy vegetables • Or 75g (3oz) if cooked or chopped • A large bowl of salad
Protein	• 50–75g (2–3oz) lean meat, fish or poultry • 1 egg • 75g (3oz) dried beans • 50g (2oz) nuts and seeds
Dairy	• 225ml (8fl oz) milk or yogurt • 50g (2oz) cheese

There's nothing wrong with eating a bit of fat – it is vital for fat-soluble vitamins. All types of fat carry a lot of calories but saturates (found in meat, full fat dairy and hydrogenated vegetable oils) and particularly manufactured trans fats are believed to be the most harmful as they affect our cholesterol balance. Trans fats have been used in baked goods and snacks for many years as a cheap solution to prolonging the shelf life of products. Trans fats (manufactured from liquid vegetable oils) are believed to reduce levels of good cholesterol and increase the levels of bad cholesterol in our bodies.

Junk foods such as biscuits, fizzy drinks, crisps, ready meals and takeaways are bursting with either fats and sugars or both – far more than you would ever put in your own cooking, plus many contain lots of salt. While only a saint would spurn them altogether, every time you turn down processed food in favour of something more wholesome, you are doing both yourself and your family a favour – though they might not think so at the time. One compromise you can make is to follow healthy eating guidelines for four out of every five days. This is known as the 80/20 rule, because you stick to healthy principles for 80 per cent of the time.

Other tips for reducing your food intake from this group include:
• Butter bread sparingly (and not at all for sandwiches – let the filling moisten the bread).
• Leave the sugar bowl off the breakfast table altogether.
• Snack on fresh and dried fruits, walnuts and pistachios.
• Try fruit and herbal teas – you won't add sugar or reach for a biscuit to dunk. Better still, stick with water (we should drink 1.5–2 litres (2½–3½ pints) of liquids a day).

Cooking healthily

Many of the pre-packaged foods on the supermarket shelves contain colourings and preservatives and also high quantities of sugar and salt. So rather than reach for a ready meal, ideally we should try to cook from scratch (it's fun and the results taste much better) so we know exactly what we are feeding ourselves and our families. If you do buy anything that is pre-prepared, check the labels carefully and shop healthily.

The health shop
• Plan the next few days' meals and stick to your list.
• Eat a healthy snack before you go to the supermarket: you'll be less tempted by the treats.
• Supermarkets know that customers reward themselves for buying healthy foods by popping high-fat and sugary treats in the trolley, so they position these 'gifts' at eye level where you'll see them. Stick to your list and resist!
• Read the label. 'Lower fat' just means less than there was and can still be pretty high. Low-fat foods can be choc-a-bloc with sugar, extra starch (check the calorie content) and salt.

Shops are designed to tempt us to purchase more. Stay in charge: plan your meals, write a list, and stick to it.

Push for fibre

Another important element in the diet is fibre, which stays solid in the body, thus helping the gut to push food along and preventing constipation. Lack of fibre in the diet (which is common) has been linked with bowel cancer. High fibre foods include fruit and vegetables, wholegrain cereals and wholemeal bread.

Vitamins and minerals

We need a range of vitamins and minerals to help our bodies work properly. Some are absorbed with the help of water; others need to be consumed with fats so that we can digest the nutrients. A balanced diet will supply them and get them into our system. Smoking hinders the absorption of Vitamin C, while tea, coffee and bran have a similar effect on iron.

Vitamins

Vitamin	Good for	Found in
Vitamin A (including beta-carotene and retinol)	Eyesight, fighting infection, growth, healthy skin, bones and teeth	Liver, fish liver oils, kidneys, dairy produce, eggs, dark green and yellow vegetables and fruit
B complex vitamins (including thiamin, riboflavin and folic acid)	Digestion, healthy skin, nails and hair, the nervous system	Wholegrain cereals and yeast extract, lean meat, tofu, green leafy vegetables, dairy produce, bananas
Vitamin C	Absorbing iron, body tissues, healing, skin, fighting infection	Citrus fruits, dark leafy vegetables, kiwi fruit, red berries
Vitamin D	Absorbing calcium, healthy bones and teeth, the immune system	Oily fish, dairy produce, made by our bodies through sunlight
Vitamin E	Healing of tissue, the immune system, red blood cells, skin	Vegetable oils, wheatgerm, wholegrain cereals, egg yolks, seeds and nuts
Vitamin K	Blood clotting, bones	Dairy produce including live bio yogurt, dark leafy vegetables, egg yolks, fish oils

Minerals

Mineral	Good for	Found in
Calcium	Bones, teeth and nails, heart, muscles, the nervous system	Milk, cheese, yogurt, tinned fish when bones are eaten, bread, seeds, soya
Iron	Circulating oxygen, red blood cells	Liver, red meats, fish, dried fruits, e.g. apricots, wholegrain cereals, green leafy vegetables, tomatoes
Magnesium	Digestion, heart, the nervous system	Carrots, citrus fruits, garlic, green leafy vegetables, nuts and seeds, onions, tomatoes
Selenium	Fighting disease, the immune system	Liver, lean meats, fish and seafood, egg yolks, nuts
Zinc	Digestion, the immune system	Lean meat, dairy foods, shell fish, nuts and seeds, wholegrain cereals

It is said that the family that eats together, stays together. So the family that cooks together as well must be even stronger! On a serious note, getting involved in cooking makes people aware of what goes into food – and just how unnatural are some of the ingredients of many processed foods.

• Ingredients are listed on labels in order of amount. So if the first ingredient is sugar and all the healthy stuff appears way down the list, put it back on the shelf: it's a glorified sweet.
• Other words used for sugar are sucrose, glucose, fructose, maltose, hydrolysed starch, invert sugar, corn syrup and honey. Sometimes you'll see more than one of these words in the same list of ingredients. That means it's fizzing with sugar.
• Look for the fat content and type of fat. Minimise consumption of saturated fat and try to avoid hydrogenated fats.
• Don't buy high-fat snacks such as crisps and biscuits: if they're not in the house, you can't eat them. Healthier alternatives include fresh and dried fruit, walnuts, pistachios and homemade muffins (see page 31).

The magic chef
Be a kitchen magician and make some of the fat, sugar and salt disappear! Plan meals to avoid high fat content. For example:
• Opt for comforting baked potatoes rather than chips.
• Reduce the meat content of stews, adding vegetables, pulses or beans.

• Cook pies with one crust (a lid or base) rather than two.
• Use lemon juice or rice wine vinegar and soy sauce as a salad dressing.
• If people in your family aren't keen on vegetables, sneak them in by adding puréed vegetables to dishes such as Bolognese sauce. They'll never know! This also adds flavour, allowing you to reduce the salt added.

Ways to cook healthily
• Trim excess fat off meat, and remove chicken skin, before you cook it.
• Frying and roasting are fat-heavy cooking methods: consider grilling, baking, poaching or steaming instead.
• For frying or searing, use a non-stick pan with a heavy base. Minimise the fat you add by using an oil spray, or by measuring out the oil by the spoonful rather than just pouring some in.
• Minced or diced meat has enough fat to cook in its own juices: you don't need to add fat. You can also drain off its fat once it is cooked.
• Stir-fries needn't be full of fat: cut fish or meat and vegetables into small pieces and use a large wok or pan with a little oil. The trick is to keep the food moving around to stop it sticking, and

Heavy drinker
Drinking too much alcohol is bad for your health and your figure. Alcohol contains sugar and other carbohydrates. Half a pint of beer, lager or cider contains 90 calories, while a glass of wine has 75 and a pub measure of spirits has 50 calories. Each of these drinks is equal to one unit, and doctors suggest a weekly maximum of 14 units for women and 21 for men, while a couple of alcohol-free days per week are recommended.

not to add too much sauce, as this produces soggy vegetables and stewed, tougher meat.

• When roasting, cook the meat on a rack to allow the fat to drop away, and use a gravy sauce mix rather than using the roasting fat.

• Dry-roasted potatoes are delicious and lower in fat: parboil them, brush or spray with oil, then bake.

• In cheese sauces, use small quantities of stronger flavoured cheese, such as Parmesan or extra-mature Cheddar.

• If a sauce recipe calls for adding cream or cream of coconut, try fromage frais or yogurt instead, which should be added at the end of cooking and not allowed to boil.

A way of life

Our nutritional needs change throughout our lives. Young people need more energy foods to fuel their growth: calorie intake should peak in the teenage years to aid growth spurts and the onset of puberty. Surveys suggest children eat too many sweets and salty snacks and not enough vegetables, fruit, lean meat and dairy foods while they are also less active than youngsters in the past. Young children learn by copying, so parents need to act as healthy role models and eat a variety of foods and not over-do snacks and fizzy drinks. Eating together is also a social activity that fosters healthy relationships.

If adults have too much food and/or exercise too little, they will store the excess energy as fat and put on weight. As we age, reductions in muscle strength and in physical activity lessen the need for calories, but our vitamin and mineral needs don't change – indeed, they can even increase if our bodies absorb them less efficiently. Some habits that stimulate good digestion include:

Salt it away

We all need some salt (sodium chloride) in our diet – about 6g a day (roughly a teaspoonful). Too much salt risks raising your blood pressure and causing heart problems and most of our needs are met through our everyday diet: we don't need to add it at the table. Indeed, many foods, such as biscuits and breakfast cereals, have lots of salt in them, which you can't always detect. We get used to the taste of salt and if you just stop using it, food can seem unpleasantly bland. The best way to cut down is to reduce it gradually while your palate adjusts. Low salt doesn't have to mean low flavour: try these ways to make food tastier:

• Use plenty of herbs – fresh tastes best and should be added just before serving.

• Marinade meat in savoury liquid, such as wine or lemon juice and spices.

• Garlic, ginger and chillies will pep up a meal, and can be chopped and frozen in small quantities to use when you feel like including them in a dish.

• Red wine is great in stews and casseroles, while white wine adds flavour to sauces and risotto; simply freeze small quantities in an ice cube tray.

• Add some mustard, chutney, flavoured vinegar or oyster sauce, although remember some contain salt and a little adds a lot of flavour.

• Lemon juice really boosts fish and seafood flavours.

• Don't put the salt pot on the table.

• Drinking plenty of water.

• Eating slowly and chewing food well: it gives your body time to tell you when it is full.

• Topping up fuel levels between meals with healthy snacks.

• Avoiding binging on sugary foods because your body will start craving that sugar 'high'.

• If possible, walking or cycling short journeys.

We can all stay healthy (and still enjoy food!) by eating properly and exercising regularly, working to these guidelines:

• Ensure you eat a balanced, varied diet of foods you enjoy.

• Keep fat intake to a minimum.

• Eat plenty of fresh food.

• Cut down on sugary drinks and foods.

• Drink alcohol sensibly.

Cook's information

All of the recipes in this book give measurements in both metric and imperial but we have supplied conversion tables here, should you need them when working with other recipes. We have also given a few tables of information that you may find useful.

Dry weight conversions

Recommended grams (g)	Imperial ounces (oz)
15	½
25	1
50	2
75	3
110	4 (¼lb)
150	5
175	6
200	7
225	8 (½lb)
250	9
275	10
300	11
350	12 (¾lb)
375	13
400	14
425	15
450	16 (1lb)
500	1lb 2oz
680	1½lb
750	1lb 10oz
900	2lb

These quantities are not exact, but they have been calculated to give proportionately correct measurements.

Spoon measures

1 tablespoon	= 3 level teaspoons
1 level tablespoon	= 15ml
1 level teaspoon	= 5ml

If greater accuracy is not required:

1 rounded teaspoon = 2 level teaspoons

1 heaped teaspoon = 3 level teaspoons or 1 level tablespoon

Seasoning and use of ingredients

• Some of the recipes in this book say season to taste. If you are happy with the flavour of the dish, then simply leave out salt and pepper, but if you feel it needs seasoning, just add a little at a time.

• Some recipes state that they are suitable for vegetarians; ensure that you use vegetarian cheese or yogurt if cooking these dishes for non-meat eaters.

• Raw eggs should not be eaten by 'at risk' groups, such as pregnant women, babies and elderly people.

• Recipes using nuts or nut oil are not suitable for young children or those with an allergic reaction to nuts.

• Always wash fruit and vegetables before using them.

Liquid conversions

Metric (ml)	Imperial (fl oz)	US cups
15	½	1 tbsp (level)
30	1	⅛
60	2	¼
90	3	⅜
125	4	½
150	5 (¼ pint)	⅔
175	6	¾
225	8	1
300	10 (½ pint)	1¼
350	12	1½
450	16	2
500	18	2¼
600	20 (1 pint)	2½
900	1½ pints	3¾
1 litre	1¾ pints	1 quart (4 cups)
1.25 litres	2 pints	1¼ quarts
1.5 litres	2½ pints	3 US pints
2 litres	3½ pints	2 quarts

568ml = 1 UK pint (20fl oz)   16fl oz = 1 US pint

These quantities are not exact, but they have been calculated to give proportionately correct measurements.

Oven temperatures

°C	°F	Gas mark	Description
110	225	¼	cool
120/130	250	½	cool
140	275	1	very low
150	300	2	very low
160/170	325	3	low to moderate
180	350	4	moderate
190	375	5	moderately hot
200	400	6	hot
220	425	7	hot
230	450	8	hot
240	475	9	very hot

Guide to recommended equivalent settings, not exact conversions. Always refer to your cooker instruction book.

Steaming times: vegetables

Vegetable	Steaming time
Asparagus	5–7 mins
Beansprouts	3–4 mins
Beetroot (sliced)	5–7 mins
Broccoli (florets)	5–7 mins
Brussels sprouts	5–7 mins
Cabbage (chopped)	4–6 mins
Cauliflower (florets)	5–7 mins
Carrots (thickly sliced)	5–7 mins
Courgettes (sliced)	3–5 mins
Green beans	5–7 mins
Leeks	5–8 mins
Mangetout peas	3–5 mins
Peas	3–5 mins
Potatoes (cubed)	5–7 mins

Times given are for steaming from when the water has started to boil.

Estimated average requirements

Estimated average requirements (EARs) are the amount of nutrients or energy required each day for the average adult.

	Women	Men
Calories	1900	2550
Saturated fat	11g	11g
Salt	< 6g	< 6g
Fibre	18g	18g

Roasting times: meat

Set oven temperature to 180°C/350°F/Gas 4.

	Cooking time per 450g/1lb	Extra cooking time
Beef		
Rare	20 mins	20 mins
Medium	25 mins	25 mins
Well done	30 mins	30 mins
Lamb		
Medium	25 mins	25 mins
Well done	30 mins	30 mins
Pork		
Medium	30 mins	30 mins
Well done	35 mins	35 mins

Let the cooked meat rest for 5–15 minutes before carving to allow the juices to be reabsorbed and to make carving easier.

Grilling times: fish

Type of fish	Grilling time
Cod (steak)	5–6 mins each side
Dover sole (whole)	4–6 mins each side
Dover sole (fillet)	2–3 mins each side
Halibut (steak)	5–6 mins each side
Herring (whole)	4–5 mins each side
Mackerel (whole)	6–7 mins each side
Monkfish (steak)	5–6 mins each side
Plaice (whole)	4–6 mins each side
Plaice (fillet)	2–3 mins each side
Salmon (steak)	5–6 mins each side
Tuna (steak)	1–2 mins each side

Times given for fish weighing approximately 175–225g (6–8oz).

Roasting times: poultry

	Oven temperature	Cooking time per 450g/1lb	Extra cooking time	Resting time
Chicken	200°C/400°F/Gas 6	20 mins	30 mins	15 mins
Turkey (stuffed weight)				
small (under 6kg/13lb)	200°C/400°F/Gas 6	12 mins	20 mins	30 mins
large	180°C/350°F/Gas 4	16 mins	—	30 mins
Duck	200°C/400°F/Gas 6 for 45 mins then 180°C/350°F/Gas 4	35 mins	—	15 mins

Sinless
SNACKS

Preparation time **15 minutes**
Cooking time **10 minutes**
Calories per portion **214 Kcal**
Fat per portion **2g**
of which saturated **0.8g**
Serves **2**
Suitable for vegetarians

Pitta crisps with tzatziki

A modern version of Melba toast, these pitta bread fingers curl up during cooking, which makes them ideal for scooping up lots of the delicious dip. This savoury snack is a really tasty way to boost your calcium intake.

Cook's tip

For mildly spicy crisps, sprinkle the pitta bread fingers with a little ground coriander before you cook them.

Wholemeal pitta breads 2
Olive oil spray 2–3 bursts
Cucumber ¼, deseeded and finely chopped
Mint 2–3 tbsp chopped leaves
Low fat natural yogurt 150g (5oz)

1 Preheat the oven to 200°C/400°F/Gas 6. Cut the pitta bread into fingers, then split each finger in half to give 2 pieces. Spread the fingers on a baking sheet, cut side up. Season to taste with freshly ground black pepper and spray with 2–3 bursts of the olive oil spray.

2 Bake the pittas in the centre of the oven for 5–10 minutes, or until they start to curl up and turn golden.

3 Remove them from the oven and turn over, then return them to the oven for a further 2–3 minutes, to ensure they have dried out and will be crisp.

4 To make the dip, stir the cucumber and most of the chopped mint into the yogurt. Season to taste. Put the tzatziki in a bowl, garnish it with the remaining chopped mint and serve with the warm pitta crisps.

Preparation time **15 minutes plus 30 minutes chilling**
Calories per portion **55 Kcal**
Fat per portion **0.4g**
of which saturated **0g**
Serves **4**
Suitable for vegetarians

Sweet & sour vegetable dip

Packed full of crunch and flavour, this attractive dip is perfect to serve at a party. However, it is just as good as a tangy snack when you need something to nibble. Not only is it low in fat, it is also packed with vitamins A and C, crucial for a healthy immune system.

Cook's tip

It is worth chilling this dip for a short while as it allows the flavours to develop. It can also be prepared well in advance of serving.

Orange pepper ½, deseeded and finely chopped
Green pepper ½, deseeded and finely chopped
Spring onions 4, trimmed and finely chopped
Pineapple 2 slices, cored and finely chopped

Bean shoots 25g (1oz), roughly chopped
Chopped tomatoes with garlic 400g can
White wine vinegar 1 tbsp
Reduced salt soy sauce 1 tbsp
Caster sugar 2 tsp
Chilli sauce ¼ tsp

1 Place the chopped peppers, spring onions, pineapple and bean shoots in a bowl and stir in the chopped tomatoes, vinegar, soy sauce, sugar and chilli sauce. Cover and chill for 30 minutes.

2 Transfer to a serving bowl and serve with mini rice cakes and vegetable crudités.

Preparation time **2 minutes**
Cooking time **5 minutes**
Calories per portion **123 Kcal**
Fat per portion **2g**
of which saturated **0g**
Serves **2**
Suitable for vegetarians

Chilli corn

Super-quick to prepare and scrumptious to snack on, this dish is perfect for when you are feeling peckish. Discovered by Columbus in 1492, corn on the cob is a delicious way to get one of your five-a-day plus a useful fibre-fix.

Cook's tip

If you don't have a microwave oven, then cook the corn in boiling water for 5–10 minutes, until it's just tender, and then spread with the chilli sauce before serving.

Corn on cob 2, husks removed
Sweet chilli dipping sauce 2–3 tbsp, plus extra to serve

1 Wash the corn well and cut each cob into three pieces.

2 Lay out two pieces of cling film and put three pieces of corn on each. Spread the chilli dipping sauce over the cobs and wrap securely in cling film.

3 Place both cobs in a microwave oven and cook on full power for 4–5 minutes, or until the corn just feels tender. Remove them from the oven and leave them to cool for a minute before unwrapping, taking care as they will be very hot as the steam escapes. Serve immediately with extra sweet chilli dipping sauce.

Preparation time **10 minutes**
Cooking time **10–15 minutes**
Calories per croustard **26 Kcal**
Fat per croustard **1g**
of which saturated **0.3g**
Makes **18 croustards**

Quick Parmesan croustards

Perfect for those crisp-craving occasions, this is a satisfyingly savoury snack that can be enjoyed on its own or as part of a buffet selection. If you have a larger gathering, simply buy a bigger baguette. Make the croustards in advance – they will keep for a couple of weeks.

Cook's tip

When cold, the croustards may be stored in an airtight container for up to 2 weeks in a cool, dry cupboard.

Small, individual-size baguette approximately 20cm (8in) long
Garlic 1 clove, peeled and crushed (optional)

Olive oil 1 tbsp
Parmesan cheese 15g (½oz), finely grated
Small basil leaves to garnish, optional

1 Preheat the oven to 180°C/350°F/Gas 4. Cutting diagonally, divide the baguette into 18 thin slices, each approximately 4mm (⅛in) thick. Blend together the garlic and olive oil, and very lightly brush it over both sides of each slice of bread.

2 Place the slices on a baking tray in a single layer and sprinkle the Parmesan evenly over each one. Season to taste with black pepper. Bake the croustards in the oven for 10–15 minutes until crisp and lightly browned. Serve warm or cold with a little bowl of olives and small basil leaves scattered over.

Preparation time **15 minutes plus 30 minutes chilling**
Calories per cheese ball **59 Kcal**
Fat per cheese ball **5g**
of which saturated **1.3g**
Makes **8 cheese balls**
Suitable for vegetarians

Cashew cheese balls

Cashew nuts are an excellent source of minerals and essential nutrients, including iron, copper and potassium. Here, combined with cream cheese, they have the bonus of calcium, essential for strong teeth. They are easily portable, so pop one or two in your lunchbox.

Cook's tip

For a really speedy snack, omit the cashew nuts and use the cheese mixture as a dip with crunchy raw vegetables.

Light soft cream cheese 110g (4oz)
Finely chopped coriander or chives 1 tbsp, plus extra unchopped to garnish

Curry powder 1 tsp
Cashew nuts 50g (2oz), chopped

1 In a bowl, mix together the cream cheese, coriander or chives and curry powder. Refrigerate for 30 minutes, to allow the mixture to become firm.

2 Roll the mixture into walnut-sized balls and then roll in the chopped nuts. Chill for a further 30 minutes. Eat alone as a snack or serve with salad for lunch.

Preparation time **20 minutes**
Cooking time **25-30 minutes**
Calories per flapjack **167 Kcal**
Fat per flapjack **12g**
of which saturated **4.7g**
Makes **12 flapjacks**
Suitable for vegetarians + freezing

Cheese flapjacks

Beware, as these are very moreish! They make an interesting, and healthier, alternative to the traditional sweet flapjack. Oats contain complex carbohydrates, which are released slowly to sustain energy levels and keep hunger pangs at bay.

Cook's tip

These are great to make and keep in an airtight container in the cupboard. If anyone in the family fancies a savoury snack, they are the perfect healthy alternative to crisps.

Butter or margarine 50g (2oz)
Cashew nuts 50g (2oz)
Macadamia nuts 25g (1oz), halved
Carrot 1 large, peeled and grated
Double Gloucester cheese 110g (4oz), grated

Porridge oats 150g (5oz)
Dried mixed herbs ½ tsp
Egg 1, beaten

1 Preheat the oven to 180°C/350°F/Gas 4. Melt the butter in the microwave or a saucepan. Remove from the heat and then add the nuts, carrot, cheese, oats, herbs and egg. Mix well.

2 Grease a 20cm (8in) round pie tin. Spoon the mixture into the tin and press down well. Bake for 25–30 minutes, until golden brown. Leave in the tin to cool and then cut into 12 wedges. Serve cold as a snack.

Preparation time **15 minutes**
Cooking time **20 minutes**
Calories per portion **70 Kcal**
Fat per portion **4.2g**
of which saturated **2.4g**
Serves **6**
Suitable for vegetarians

Mushroom pâté

Ideal for an evening snack, this pâté is easy to make and delicious to eat. It contains calcium and magnesium. Serve the pâté with a variety of crunchy vegetables or a small chunk of seeded bread.

Cook's tip

Look out for cartons of budget mushrooms of mixed shapes and sizes – it doesn't matter what shape the mushrooms are as they are going to be puréed.

Vegetable stock 300ml (½ pint)
Onion 1, peeled and chopped
Celery 2 sticks, chopped
Garlic 1 clove, peeled and chopped

Mushrooms 300g (11oz), wiped and chopped
Chopped thyme 1 tbsp, or 1 tsp dried
Light soft cream cheese 200g (7oz)

1 Bring the stock to the boil and add the onion, celery and garlic. Reduce the heat and cover the pan and simmer the vegetables gently for 10 minutes. Add the mushrooms and thyme and simmer for a further 8–10 minutes, or until the vegetables are soft.

2 There should just be a small amount of liquid remaining in the pan with the vegetables. If there is a lot of liquid, then remove the lid and boil the mixture rapidly to boil off the excess. Remove the pan from the heat and leave the mixture to cool.

3 Tip the mushroom mixture into the bowl of a food processor and purée until smooth. Then add the cream cheese and purée again until the cheese is well mixed in. Season to taste with salt and pepper. Transfer the mixture to a covered bowl and keep it chilled until serving. The pâté will keep in the fridge for up to 2 days.

Preparation time **10 minutes plus
1 hour chilling**
Calories per portion **93 Kcal**
Fat per portion **5g**
of which saturated **1.3g**
Serves **6**

Sardine pâté with vegetables

This recipe makes the perfect pre-dinner snack when cooking for friends. Packed full of omega-3 essential fats and selenium, it epitomises a 'sinless snack'. Mackerel and tuna are also very healthy, so use these if you prefer.

Cook's tip

This recipe works equally well with other canned fish, such as tuna, salmon, mackerel and pilchards.

Sardines 120g can, drained
Light soft cream cheese 75g (3oz)
Sun-dried tomato purée 1 tbsp
Lemon juice 1 tbsp
Worcestershire sauce 1 tbsp

Carrots 3 large, peeled and cut into crudités
Celery 2 sticks, cut into crudités
Cherry tomatoes 12

1 Put the sardines into a bowl and mash well with a fork. Add the cream cheese, tomato purée, lemon juice and Worcestershire sauce. Season to taste with black pepper and mix well.

2 Cover and chill for at least an hour. Serve with the vegetables and tomatoes as a speedy and healthy snack.

Preparation time **15 minutes**
Calories per skewer **29 Kcal**
Fat per skewer **0.4g**
of which saturated **0.1g**
Makes **8 skewers**

Melon, cucumber & ham skewers

Refreshing and light, these skewers make a great snack. For extra flavour, sprinkle with freshly chopped mint or drizzle with a little raspberry vinegar. Each skewer provides a quick fix of protein and fibre to fill a gap between meals.

Cook's tip

You can make mini versions of these simple skewers by cutting the ingredients into small pieces and threading onto cocktail sticks. They will then make bite-sized canapés for a party.

Green melon (Galia) ½
Orange melon (Charantais) ½
Cucumber ½
Wafer-thin lean ham 6 slices

1 Scoop out the seeds from the melon halves, then slice off the skin and cut the flesh into pieces approximately 2cm (¾in) square.

2 Using a vegetable peeler, remove the skin from the cucumber, and cut in half lengthways. Cut into pieces slightly thinner than the melon.

3 Cut each slice of ham into strips. Thread pieces of melon, cucumber and ham onto eight bamboo skewers, winding the ham between the melon and cucumber pieces. Cover and chill until required.

Preparation time **20/10 minutes**
(fresh/dried fruit)
Calories per portion **43/54 Kcal**
(fresh/dried fruit)
Fat per portion **0.1g** (fresh/dried fruit)
of which saturated **0g** (fresh/dried fruit)
Makes **12/18** (fresh/dried fruit)
Suitable for vegetarians

Fresh & dried fruit nibbles

Ideal for moments when you crave something sweet, these fruity kebabs are full of vitamins and minerals, in particular the dried fruit nibbles, which are a good source of iron. Limit yourself to only two or three dried fruit nibbles as they do contain quite a lot of sugar.

Cook's tip

Avoid using fresh fruits such as apples, pears, peaches and bananas as these tend to discolour and will not keep as well as those suggested.

Fresh fruit selection
Pineapple ½ large, skinned and cored
Mango 1, halved, stoned and skinned
Melon 175g (6oz) prepared flesh
Black grapes 175g (6oz)
White grapes 175g (6oz)

Dried fruit selection
Agen prunes 9 large, pitted and halved
Medjool dates 9 large, pitted and quartered
Ready-to-eat dried apricots 9 large, halved

1 To make the fresh fruit nibbles, cut the pineapple, mango and melon into 2cm (¾in) cubes. Wash and dry the grapes.

2 Thread the fruits alternately onto wooden skewers, and then place them in a plastic container. Cover with cling film and a tight-fitting lid and refrigerate – they will keep for 2 to 3 days.

3 For the dried fruit nibbles, thread all the prepared fruits alternately onto cocktail sticks and then place in a plastic container.

4 Cover with a tight-fitting lid and store in the refrigerator, where they will keep for several weeks. Chilling the fruits gives them a more refreshing taste. Soft, dried figs may also be used, if wished.

Preparation time **5 minutes**
Calories per smoothie **147 Kcal**
Fat per smoothie **2g**
of which saturated **1.3g**
Makes **2 smoothies**
Suitable for vegetarians

Two berry smoothie

This smoothie is nutritious and quick to make for breakfast or for an afternoon 'pick me up' for anyone in the family. Full of vitamins and minerals, berries are rich in antioxidants, which help to protect against cancer.

Cook's tip

For less washing-up, put the yogurt and fruit in a large jug and use a stick blender to purée. Then whisk in the milk with a little iced water.

Low fat natural yogurt 150g (5oz)
Banana 1 really ripe
Blueberries and raspberries mixed 150g (5oz)

Semi-skimmed milk 150ml (¼ pint)
Ice cubes 4, optional

1 Put all the ingredients, except the ice cubes, in a food processor and whiz them together until they are smooth smooth.

2 Add the ice cubes and blend for a further 20–30 seconds until the ice is roughly crushed. Pour into tall chilled glasses and serve immediately.

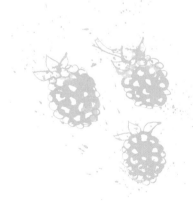

Preparation time **5 minutes**
Calories per portion **203 Kcal**
Fat per portion **15g**
of which saturated **4.1g**
Serves **2**
Suitable for vegetarians

Café noisette

Here is a deliciously grown-up milkshake full of calcium, which is essential for healthy bones and teeth. This chilled drink is perfect served mid-morning on sunny days as a refreshing alternative to a cup of coffee.

Cook's tip

For a sweeter drink, add 2 teaspoons of sugar or granulated sweetener to the coffee granules before you add the boiling water.

Coffee granules 2 tsp
Boiling water 4 tbsp
Chopped hazelnuts 2 tbsp
Semi-skimmed milk 300ml (½ pint)
Single cream 2 tbsp
Cocoa powder for sprinkling

1 Dissolve the coffee granules in the boiling water and pour into a food processor.

2 Gently toast the hazelnuts in a pan over a low heat for around 5 minutes and then spoon into the processor. Add the milk, put on the lid and then blend everything together.

3 Pour into two glasses and add 1 tablespoon of cream to each. Sprinkle with a dusting of cocoa powder and serve immediately.

Preparation time **5 minutes**
Cooking time **5 minutes**
Calories per portion **128 Kcal**
Fat per portion **1g**
of which saturated **0.1g**
Serves **1**
Suitable for vegetarians

Spiced fruity crumpet

Really easy to make and very low in fat, this snack is great for anyone in a hurry who needs a little something to keep them going. Use fresh, or for real speed, canned pineapple, which is rich in manganese, a trace mineral that contributes to energy production.

Cook's tip

This simple idea can be varied to suit your taste. Try other fruits, such as plums, peaches and mango, and with different spices, like cinnamon and nutmeg.

Pineapple 1 slice
Ground ginger ½ tsp
Crumpet 1
Honey ½ tsp

1 Place the slice of pineapple on a board and rub one side all over with the ground ginger.

2 Preheat the grill to medium or dry heat a ridged frying pan. Cook the pineapple slice along with the crumpet under the grill or on the pan for 5–6 minutes, turning each once, until the crumpet is hot on both sides.

3 Pop the pineapple on top of the crumpet and drizzle with the honey.

Preparation time **2 minutes**
Calories per portion **113 Kcal**
Fat per portion **2g**
of which saturated **1g**
Serves **2**
Suitable for vegetarians

Strawberry 'cream tea'

Cream tea, what a decadent delight! This version is low in fat and sugar and so can be eaten guilt-free. The rice cakes make the perfect, crispy base for a fruity topping, creating a light, yet scrumptious snack.

Cook's tip

Look out for high fibre rice cakes and choose a conserve with a low sugar content. As the sugar content may be low, keep the jar refrigerated after opening.

Strawberry conserve 2 tbsp
Rice cakes 2
Light soft cream cheese 2 tbsp

Icing sugar 2 tsp
Strawberries 3–4, sliced

1 Spread the strawberry conserve over the rice cakes.

2 Mix together the cream cheese and icing sugar and spoon on top of the conserve. Top with the strawberry slices and serve immediately.

Preparation time **15 minutes plus 4 hours soaking**
Cooking time **50–60 minutes**
Calories per slice **116 Kcal**
Fat per slice **1g**
of which saturated **0.2g**
Makes **12 slices**
Suitable for vegetarians + freezing

Orchard fruit loaf

Put your feet up for half an hour, relax and enjoy a cup of tea and a slice of this delicious fruit loaf. It is important to take time out to unwind totally and forget the stresses and strains of everyday life.

Cook's tip

Try different combinations of colourful, different textured exotic fruits for this recipe, both for the dried fruits and the fruit spread.

Ready-to-eat dried fruit, e.g apricots, prunes, apples, cranberries and pears 225g (8oz), roughly chopped
Low sugar or no added sugar orange, lemon and pineapple squash 4 tbsp

Half sugar seville orange fruit spread 4 tbsp
Egg 1 large
Self-raising flour 250g (9oz)

1 Put the dried fruits in a large bowl. Make the fruit squash up to 225ml (8fl oz) with water and pour over the fruits. Stir well, cover and leave until the fruits have absorbed most of the liquid (about 4 hours).

2 Preheat the oven to 180°C/350°F/Gas 4. Carefully strip line a 1kg (2lb) loaf tin with baking parchment.

3 Beat the fruit spread and egg into the soaked fruit, and then sift in the flour and mix well.

4 Spoon the mixture into the loaf tin. Smooth the top and bake for 50–60 minutes until a skewer, when inserted, comes out clean. If the loaf is browning too much towards the end of its cooking time, cover with foil. When cooked, remove from the oven and leave to cool in the tin for 15 minutes. Then carefully tip out of the tin, peel away the paper and leave the loaf to cool on a wire rack. Cut into slices for serving.

Preparation time **10 minutes**
Cooking time **25 minutes plus cooling**
Calories per muffin **246 Kcal**
Fat per muffin **5g**
of which saturated **0.9g**
Makes **10 muffins**
Suitable for vegetarians + freezing

Carrot & ginger muffins

These muffins are moist, full of flavour and topped with a creamy light frosting. They are perfect for picnics as you can pop them into a box and take them with you (just take the fromage frais in a separate pot). A healthy treat to enjoy in the great outdoors.

Cook's tip

For more fibre, use self-raising wholemeal flour in place of the ordinary self-raising flour.

Self-raising flour 225g (8oz)
Ground ginger 2 tsp, plus extra to serve
Light brown sugar 175g (6oz)
Carrots 225g (8oz), peeled and grated
Stem ginger in syrup 3 pieces, drained and chopped

Sultanas 50g (2oz)
Eggs 2, beaten
Corn oil 3 tbsp
Freshly squeezed orange juice 6 tbsp
Low fat natural fromage frais 225g (8oz), plus extra to serve
Icing sugar 2 tbsp

1 Preheat the oven to 180°C/350°F/Gas 4. Line ten deep cup muffin tins with paper muffin cases. Sift the flour and ground ginger into a mixing bowl. Stir in the sugar, carrots, chopped ginger and sultanas.

2 Make a well in the centre and gradually blend in the eggs, oil and orange juice to form a thick batter. Divide between the muffin cases, smooth the tops and bake in the oven for about 25 minutes until risen and golden. Transfer the muffins to a wire rack to cool.

3 For the frosting, place the fromage frais in a bowl and sieve in the icing sugar. Mix well. Cover and chill until ready to serve.

4 Serve each muffin with a dollop of fromage frais on top and a light dusting of ground ginger. Best eaten within 2 days of baking; store in an airtight container.

Preparation time **20 minutes**
Cooking time **10 minutes**
Calories per bun **204 Kcal**
Fat per bun **12g**
of which saturated **2.5g**
Makes **10 buns**
Suitable for vegetarians + freezing

Banana & chocolate buns

The perfect choice for chocaholics! Reward yourself with one of these banana flavoured buns after a swim, a walk in the local park or half an hour on your bicycle. Eating well and regular exercise go hand-in-hand after all.

Light muscovado sugar 75g (3oz)
Sunflower oil 100ml (3½fl oz)
Eggs 2
Banana 1, mashed

Self-raising flour 110g (4oz)
Cocoa 15g (½oz)
White chocolate 40g (1½oz), melted, to decorate

1 Preheat the oven to 180°C/350°F/Gas 4 and put 10 paper muffin cases into a muffin tray. Put the sugar and oil in a mixing bowl and whisk together. Add the eggs and whisk until smooth.

2 Add the banana, flour and cocoa and whisk briefly until just mixed. Spoon into the paper cases and cook for 10 minutes until well risen and the tops spring back when pressed with a fingertip. Leave to cool in the tray.

3 Transfer the buns to a serving plate and drizzle the melted white chocolate over the top with a teaspoon.

Cook's tip

Although eggs remain fresher for longer if kept in the fridge, they are best used in baking when they are at room temperature.

Preparation time **25 minutes**
Cooking time **30-35 minutes**
Calories per slice **133 Kcal**
Fat per slice **3g**
of which saturated **0.8g**
Makes **16 slices**
Suitable for vegetarians + freezing

Spiced bread pudding

Deliciously moist, this bread pudding tastes truly scrumptious but in actual fact only contains 133 calories and 0.8g of saturated fat per slice. With its wholemeal bread, it is a good source of fibre and the dried fruits supply the body with magnesium and iron.

Cook's tip

Replace the sultanas with other dried fruits, if you prefer – try blueberries, cranberries or cherries.

Wholemeal sliced bread 300g (11oz), cut into 2.5cm (1in) squares
Semi-skimmed milk 300ml (½ pint)
Egg 1, beaten
Low fat margarine 75g (3oz)

Raisins 110g (4oz)
Sultanas 50g (2oz)
Brown sugar 110g (4oz)
Ground cinnamon 1 tbsp
Grated nutmeg 1 tbsp

1 Preheat the oven to 190°C/375°F/Gas 5. Grease a square sandwich tin that measures approximately 20 x 20cm (8 x 8in).

2 Place the bread and milk in a large bowl and mix together. Leave to soak for 5 minutes, then add all of the remaining ingredients, except for 1 tablespoon of the brown sugar, and mix well. Press into the sandwich tin and sprinkle the top with the remaining brown sugar.

3 Bake for 30–35 minutes until golden brown. Remove from the oven and leave in the tin to cool and then, when cool, turn out and cut into slices.

Lunchboxes
& LIGHT LUNCHES

Preparation time **5 minutes**
Cooking time **25 minutes**
Calories per portion **109 Kcal**
Fat per portion **3g**
of which saturated **0.1g**
Serves **4**
Suitable for vegetarians

Broccoli & apple soup

This unusual soup is packed full of goodness. Broccoli contains potent antioxidants and is recognised as a cancer preventative vegetable. Apples are a good source of magnesium and also contain pectin, which helps to reduce cholesterol.

Cook's tip

Try stirring a couple of tablespoons of low fat soft cream cheese into the soup before it is puréed. It will give it an even richer flavour and velvety texture.

Spray oil a few bursts
Red or white onion 1, peeled and chopped
Dessert apples 2, peeled, cored and chopped

Vegetable stock 750ml (1¼ pints)
Broccoli 1 large head, trimmed and roughly chopped
Low fat natural fromage frais 4 tbsp
Chopped parsley to garnish, optional

1 Spray a large saucepan with spray oil and add the chopped onion and apple. Cover and cook over a low heat for 5 minutes, stirring occasionally.

2 Pour the vegetable stock into the pan and add the broccoli, reserving a little for garnishing. Bring to the boil, cover and simmer for 15 minutes.

3 Turn off the heat and season the soup with pepper to taste. Purée with a hand-held whisk or blender and then reheat, if necessary. Serve in a tureen with a swirl of fromage frais and garnished with pieces of the reserved broccoli and chopped parsley, if using.

Preparation time: **15 minutes**
Cooking time **40-50 minutes**
Calories per portion **260 Kcal**
Fat per portion **4g**
of which saturated **1g**
Serves **4**
Suitable for vegetarians + freezing

Carrot, lentil & tomato soup

A hearty soup, which is a great source of vegetable protein and a number of essential minerals. It makes the ideal lunch when out walking. Simply keep hot in a good flask and then nourish and warm yourself with a cup of soup and a chunk of wholemeal bread.

Cook's tip

For some extra kick, add 2 cloves of finely chopped garlic to the saucepan after the onion and then ½ teaspoon smoked paprika with the remaining ingredients.

Split red lentils 110g (4oz)
Large green lentils 110g (4oz)
Light olive oil ½ tbsp
Onion 1 large, peeled and finely chopped
Carrots 225g (8oz), peeled and coarsely grated

Large tomatoes 450g (1lb), roughly chopped
Vegetable stock 1.25 litres (2 pints)
Half fat crème fraîche 2 tbsp, for swirling
Chopped coriander, parsley or chives or a mixture of all three, for sprinkling

1 Put the lentils into a large sieve, rinse well under a cold, running tap and then drain thoroughly.

2 Heat the oil in a large saucepan, add the onion and cook gently until softened, but not browned.

3 Add the grated carrots, tomatoes, drained lentils and stock to the saucepan. Bring to the boil, then reduce the heat, cover the pan and cook gently for 30 minutes, or until the vegetables are softened.

4 Place a large sieve over another large saucepan, or large bowl. Pour the soup into the sieve and then, using a wooden spoon, pass the vegetables through the sieve. Discard the remaining seeds and tomato skin.

5 Season the soup to taste, then reheat until hot. If it is a little thick at this stage, add some extra stock. Pour the soup into warmed soup bowls or mugs and serve swirled with a little crème fraîche, and sprinkled with chopped coriander, parsley or chives.

Preparation time **20 minutes**
Cooking time **30 minutes**
Calories per portion **175 Kcal**
Fat per portion **9g**
of which saturated **4.8g**
Serves **4**
Suitable for vegetarians + freezing

Leek & mushroom soup

Leeks have been used for millennia in cooking. They appear in Egyptian tomb paintings and were highly regarded by the Romans, who introduced the vegetable to Britain. Regular consumption of leek has been shown to reduce the risk of some cancers.

Cook's tip

For smooth soup, purée everything in a food processor, reheat and serve garnished with the chives.

Butter or margarine 25g (1oz)
Leeks 2, washed, trimmed and sliced
Mushrooms 225g (8oz), wiped and sliced
Semi-skimmed milk 600ml (1 pint)
Vegetable stock cubes 2

Reduced salt soy sauce 1 tbsp
Bay leaves 3
Cornflour 1 tbsp
Sherry 2 tbsp
Snipped chives to garnish

1 Melt the butter or margarine in a large saucepan and add the leeks and mushrooms. Cook for around 5 minutes, until soft.

2 Add the milk and crumbled stock cubes and then pour 300ml (½ pint) cold water into the pan. Add the soy sauce and bay leaves and bring to the boil. Cover and leave to simmer for 20 minutes.

3 Blend the cornflour with the sherry and stir into the soup. Season with pepper to taste and cook for another 2 minutes.

4 Remove the bay leaves, garnish with chives and serve with slices of bread from a wholewheat French stick.

Preparation time **15 minutes**
Cooking time **10 minutes**
Calories per portion **227 Kcal**
Fat per portion **8g**
of which saturated **4.7g**
Serves **4**

Chinese chicken soup

The two principles of Chinese cookery are 'eat to live' and 'eat for pleasure'. This recipe combines them both to create a healthy dish, full of protein, vitamins and minerals, which also tastes great!

Cook's tip

For a vegetarian soup, simply omit the chicken and use vegetable stock instead of the chicken stock. It will still taste really good.

Plain flour 2 tbsp
Butter or margarine 25g (1oz)
Chicken breasts 2 small, thinly sliced
Button mushrooms 50g (2oz), wiped and sliced
Chicken stock 300ml (½ pint)
Semi-skimmed milk 450ml (16fl oz)

Root ginger 1cm (½in) piece, peeled and grated
Reduced salt soy sauce 2 tsp
Spring onions 6, trimmed and sliced diagonally
Bean sprouts 110g (4oz)
Water chestnuts half a 220g can, drained and sliced

1 Season the flour with salt and pepper to taste and then coat the chicken in the seasoned flour.

2 Melt the butter or margarine in a large saucepan and add the chicken slices. Cook for 1 minute, stirring continuously. Add the mushrooms and any remaining flour. Then pour the stock into the pan with the milk, ginger and soy sauce. Bring to the boil, cover and leave to simmer for 2 minutes, or until the chicken is tender.

3 Add the spring onions, bean sprouts and water chestnuts and stir gently for around 1 minute. Serve immediately, while the vegetables are still crunchy.

Preparation time **10 minutes**

Cooking time **15 minutes**

Calories per portion **149 Kcal**

Fat per portion **3g**

of which saturated **0.1g**

Serves **4**

Suitable for vegetarians

Mediterranean pitta with houmous

Houmous usually has a very high fat content as it's made with lots of olive oil, but this low fat recipe uses fromage frais as a healthy alternative. This should fill you up until dinner time as it contains lots of slow energy-releasing ingredients.

Cook's tip

This recipe can be served hot as a lunchtime snack – just leave the peppers until they are cool enough to handle to peel off the skins.

Chickpeas 410g can, drained and rinsed

Garlic 1 clove, peeled

Chopped coriander 2 tbsp

Low fat natural fromage frais 200g (7oz)

Tabasco sauce dash

Red pepper 1, quartered and deseeded

Orange pepper 1, quartered and deseeded

Plum tomatoes 4, halved

Courgettes 2–3, sliced

Caster sugar pinch

Olive oil spray 4–6 bursts

Wholemeal pitta breads 4, toasted, to serve

1 To make the houmous, tip the chickpeas into the bowl of a food processor and add the garlic, coriander and fromage frais and purée until smooth. Stir in the Tabasco sauce and add seasoning to taste.

2 Turn the grill onto high to cook the vegetables. Lay the vegetables out on a grill rack, skin-side up for the peppers and cut-side up for the tomatoes. Sprinkle the sugar over the tomatoes. Spray 2–3 bursts olive oil over the courgettes.

3 Cook under the grill for 7–8 minutes until the courgettes and peppers are golden. Turn over the peppers and courgettes and spray the courgettes again with another 2–3 bursts of oil spray. Continue to cook for a further 4–5 minutes until golden.

4 Remove the vegetables from under the grill and place the red peppers in a plastic bag. Leave all vegetables to cool.

5 Scoop the tomatoes out of their skins and place in a bowl. Remove the red pepper skins and chop the flesh, and then chop the courgettes. Mix together all the vegetables, seasoning to taste.

6 Split the pitta open along one side. Fill with the vegetables, top with the houmous, and serve immediately.

Preparation time **10 minutes**
Cooking time **30 minutes**
Calories per portion **306 Kcal**
Fat per portion **5g**
of which saturated **0.9g**
Serves **2**
Suitable for vegetarians

Fruity rice salad

This fruity salad makes a refreshing change from sandwiches for lunch. Simply pack into a container with a fork or spoon to eat it with. Brown rice is high in fibre; it doesn't matter what type is used, but compare packets and choose the one with the highest fibre content.

Brown rice 110g (4oz)
Raisins 25g (1oz)
Cider vinegar 2 tbsp
Olive oil 2 tsp
Dijon mustard 1 tsp
Spring onions 4, trimmed and sliced

Green pepper 1, deseeded and chopped
Celery sticks 2, chopped
Apple 1, cored and chopped
Chopped tarragon 1 tbsp, or 1 tsp dried

1 Cook the rice in boiling water for 25–30 minutes until it is just tender, then add the raisins to the water and cook for a further 1–2 minutes. Remove the pan from the heat and strain the rice and raisins in a sieve and then run cold water through it to cool them quickly. Drain well.

2 To make the dressing, whisk together the vinegar, oil and mustard. Season the dressing to taste.

3 Tip the cooled rice and raisins into a bowl and stir in the dressing, then stir in the spring onions, green pepper, celery, apple and tarragon.

4 Keep the salad cool until serving, and then leave it to come to room temperature before eating. The salad will keep for up to 24 hours in the fridge.

Cook's tip

Take care when adding the tarragon as sometimes it can have quite a strong flavour and may be overpowering, so don't add too much.

Preparation time **10 minutes**
Cooking time **40 minutes**
Calories per portion **272 Kcal**
Fat per portion **6g**
of which saturated **3.2g**
Serves **2**
Suitable for vegetarians

Beetroot & feta-filled jackets

Jacket potatoes are good for a midday snack as they fill you up and give you energy but they need a tasty topping otherwise it's tempting to add lots of butter. Feta is lower in fat than some other cheeses and beetroot is a good source of folate and potassium.

Potatoes 2, cooked in their jackets
Feta cheese 50g (2oz)
Cooked beetroot 150g (5oz), diced
Orange or red pepper ½, deseeded and diced

Cherry tomatoes 4, quartered
Spring onions 2, trimmed and thinly sliced
Mizuna leaves and/or lamb's lettuce

1 Cut a large cross in the top of the cooked potato and squeeze it up so that the flesh starts to 'ooze' out.

2 Mix the crumbled feta with the vegetables and a sprinkling of black pepper and spoon into the hot potatoes.

3 Top with a handful of leaves and serve immediately, while the potatoes are hot.

Cook's tip

Cook your jacket potatoes in the microwave for 5-10 minutes while the oven heats up, then cook them at 200°/400°F/Gas 6 for about 30 minutes until crispy on the outside and squidgy – then you won't miss the butter!

Preparation time **5 minutes**
Cooking time **10 minutes**
Calories per portion **218 Kcal**
Fat per portion **12g**
of which saturated **3g**
Serves **2**
Suitable for vegetarians

Speedy pea & potato omelette

Quick and tasty, this omelette is a good store-cupboard standby. Frozen peas have been used in this recipe as they generally have a higher vitamin content than fresh peas, whose nutritional benefits deteriorate quickly. If you grow your own peas, use those instead.

Cook's tip

You can use any leftover cooked vegetables in this recipe; canned sweetcorn gives a good texture and other frozen vegetable mixes will give you different options.

Vegetable oil 1 tsp
Spring onions 2, trimmed and thinly sliced
Frozen peas 75g (3oz)

New potatoes 300g can, sliced
Eggs 3 large, beaten
Chopped mint leaves 1 tbsp

1 Heat the oil in a small non-stick omelette pan and cook the onions for 1 minute. Add the frozen peas and cook for a further minute. Stir in the potatoes.

2 Add the mint leaves to the beaten eggs, lower the heat for the pan and pour the eggs over the peas and potatoes. Season to taste. Stir the egg from around the sides of the pan into the centre until it sets all over. This will take about 5 minutes.

3 Preheat the grill to hot. Place the pan under the grill for 3–4 minutes until the omelette is firm and lightly golden. Remove from the pan and serve hot or cold, cut in half.

Preparation time **15 minutes**
Cooking time **30 minutes**
Calories per portion **293 Kcal**
Fat per portion **8g**
of which saturated **2.9g**
Serves **4**
Suitable for vegetarians + freezing

Pitta pizzas

Pitta breads make a quick and light pizza-style base which goes crispy in the oven. Topped with a selection of fresh vegetables, they make a filling, wholesome lunchtime snack. You can choose whichever vegetables you like best, such as artichokes or sweetcorn.

Cook's tip

If you do not have pitta breads then try this recipe using a wholewheat French stick, halved. It may take less time to cook so check from time to time.

Wholemeal pitta breads 4
Tomato ketchup 8 tsp
Garlic 1 clove, peeled and crushed, optional
Red or green pepper 1, quartered, deseeded and thinly sliced
Button mushrooms 110g (4oz), wiped and finely sliced

Spring onions 4, trimmed and finely sliced
Low fat Mozzarella 125g pack, drained
Tomatoes 4, chopped or sliced
Basil leaves about 20

1 Preheat the oven to 200°C/400°F/Gas 6. Split the pitta breads in half and put them on two heavy baking sheets. Spread each half with a teaspoon of ketchup and add a little garlic, if using, and divide the pepper, mushrooms and spring onions between them.

2 Season to taste and top with chunks of torn Mozzarella, then pieces of tomato and half the basil leaves, torn.

3 Cook for 20–23 minutes, changing the trays round in the oven half way through cooking. Serve two 'pizzas' per person garnished with basil and accompanied by lots of green salad.

Preparation time **10 minutes**
Calories per wrap **310 Kcal**
Fat per wrap **11g**
of which saturated **4.1g**
Makes **4 wraps**

Quick prawn wraps

These colourful wraps make a great addition to any lunchbox. They can be prepared a couple of hours ahead and kept in cling film in the refrigerator. Prawns provide you with vitamin B12, iodine and zinc, which are important for health.

Cook's tip

If you are using the tortilla wraps for a lunchbox, wrap in cling film rather than a paper napkin – but pack the paper napkin, too. It's easy to spill the contents of these wraps.

Light soft cream cheese 200g (7oz)
Snipped chives 3 tbsp
Peeled prawns 175g (6oz), thawed if frozen
Tabasco sauce to taste
Tortillas 4

Large plum tomatoes 3, quartered, deseeded and cut into thin strips lengthways
Rocket leaves 50g (2oz)
Watercress 50g (2oz) (trimmed weight)

1 Put the cream cheese into a bowl and stir with a fork until softened. Add the chives and prawns, season to taste with Tabasco sauce – approximately 3–4 drops – and then mix together gently.

2 Dividing the cheese mixture evenly, spread it over each tortilla. Then sprinkle each one equally with the tomato strips.

3 Scatter the rocket leaves and watercress over the tomatoes, and then roll up each tortilla tightly. Wrap each tortilla in a paper napkin and serve.

Preparation time **5 minutes**
Calories per portion **230 Kcal**
Fat per portion **5g**
of which saturated **0.7g**
Serves **2**

Tuna ciabatta

Oily fish such as tuna is very beneficial, containing essential fats, selenium and vitamins B12 and B3 (niacin). It helps to improve skin conditions, regulates hormones and contributes to maintenance of the cardiovascular system.

Cook's tip

Vegetables have the most vitamins when they are freshly picked – so look out for 'living' watercress, which you can cut just before serving, so it retains the maximum amounts of nutrients.

Tuna in spring water 200g can, drained
Light salad cream 2 tbsp
Capers 1 tbsp, rinsed and chopped if large

Horseradish sauce 1 tbsp
Plain or olive ciabatta rolls 2
Watercress to serve

1 Mix together the tuna, salad cream, capers and horseradish sauce and add seasoning to taste.

2 Split the rolls in half and spread over the tuna filling, top with the watercress, replace the top of the roll and serve immediately.

Preparation time **30 minutes**
Cooking time **10 minutes**
Calories per portion **243 Kcal**
Fat per portion **9g**
of which saturated **1.9g**
Serves **3**

Mediterranean niçoise salad

Traditional *salade niçoise* is heavily coated with a dressing made with copious amounts of olive oil. The dressing for this lighter version is made with seasoned rice vinegar, which has no fat yet still provides all the same character and flavour of this classic salad.

Fine green beans 75g (3oz), trimmed
Baby new potatoes 150g (5oz), scrubbed
Plum tomatoes 2, sliced or quartered
Red onion 1 small, peeled, thinly sliced
Canned artichoke hearts 175g (6oz), well drained and quartered
Pitted black olives 8
Anchovy fillets in olive oil 100g can, drained and cut in half lengthways

Tuna in spring water 200g can, drained
Romaine lettuce leaves 2–4, coarsely shredded
French mustard ½ tsp
Seasoned rice vinegar 2 tsp
Basil leaves a small handful, finely shredded
Eggs 2 large, hard-boiled and shelled

1 Cook the beans in boiling water for 5–6 minutes, until cooked yet still slightly crisp. Pour into a colander, rinse under a cold running tap and leave to cool.

2 Cook the potatoes in boiling water for 8–10 minutes, or until cooked. Pour into a colander, rinse under a cold running tap and leave to cool.

3 Meanwhile, place the tomatoes, onion, artichoke hearts, olives, anchovy fillets, tuna and lettuce leaves in a large salad bowl.

4 To make the dressing, put the mustard, vinegar and basil leaves into a small bowl and whisk together.

5 When cool, cut the beans into short lengths and the potatoes into thick slices. Then add both to the salad bowl.

6 Shell and slice or quarter the hard-boiled eggs. Pour the dressing over the salad and toss gently together. Arrange the eggs on top of the salad and serve immediately together with some freshly toasted slices of wholemeal bread.

Cook's tip

Buy tuna in spring water rather than in vegetable oil as it is the healthiest version of canned tuna.

Preparation time **10 minutes**
Calories per sandwich **397 Kcal**
Fat per sandwich **16g**
of which saturated **2.8g**
Makes **4 sandwiches**

Chicken & avocado salad sandwich

Avocados are a rich source of vitamin E, which is required for healthy skin and good cardiovascular health. When really ripe, avocado can be mashed and used as a tastier alternative to a low fat spread.

Cook's tip

Use fresh salmon or tuna instead of chicken in the sandwich.

Avocado 1 very ripe large
Lime or lemon juice 1 tbsp
Mint leaves 8 shredded, optional
Mixed grain bread 8 slices
Cooked chicken breast 200g (7oz), shredded

Cucumber slices 12
Baby spinach leaves 4 handfuls, rinsed and dried

1 Halve the avocado, remove the stone and scrape out the flesh onto a plate. Mash it with lime or lemon juice and add the shredded mint, if using. Spread the mashed avocado mixture over the 8 slices of bread.

2 Arrange the chicken evenly on 4 of the slices and season to taste. Put the cucumber slices on top and then pile up the spinach leaves.

3 Place the other piece of bread, avocado side down on top to make 4 sandwiches. Press them together gently and cut each into two pieces.

Preparation time **15 minutes plus
20 minutes marinating**
Cooking time **10 minutes**
Calories per portion **328 Kcal**
Fat per portion **4g**
of which saturated **0.8g**
Serves **4**

Sticky chicken with mango salsa

Chicken is low in fat but it can taste a little bland, so marinate it and add a sticky glaze to make it more exciting. This vibrant fruity salsa is full of flavour and goodness and would go well with lamb or pork too.

Cook's tip

Don't have the heat too high after the glaze goes on or it may burn. You can then pour any glaze left in the pan over the cooked chicken.

Chicken breasts 4, skinned
Limes 2, grated zest from 1, squeezed and strained juice from both
Garlic 1 or 2 cloves, peeled and crushed
Honey 2 tbsp
Tomato ketchup 1 tbsp
Reduced salt soy sauce 1 tsp
Wholegrain mustard 1 tsp

Red onion 1 small, peeled and finely diced
Mango 1, stoned, peeled and diced
Cherry tomatoes 8, chopped
Olive oil 2 tsp
Rocket or other salad leaves to serve
New potatoes about 500g /1lb 2oz, cooked, to serve

1 Cut each chicken breast into 3 long thin strips. Mix the juice from 1 lime with the crushed garlic in a shallow dish. Coat the chicken strips and leave to marinate for at least 20 minutes.

2 Mix the honey, ketchup, soy and mustard in a small bowl and set aside for glazing the chicken later.

3 To make the salsa, mix the onion, grated zest and juice from the remaining lime, diced mango and chopped tomatoes in a bowl and leave for the flavours to mingle.

4 Heat a large non-stick frying pan and add the oil. Remove the chicken from the marinade. Put in the pan and cook over a medium heat for 2 minutes, then turn over and cook for another 2 minutes.

5 Brush the glaze over the chicken breasts in the pan (use the back of a spoon or a brush) on both sides. Cook over a low heat for another 3 minutes on each side until just cooked through and sticky all over.

6 Serve with a large spoonful of salsa and salad leaves. Accompany with the potatoes and garnish with extra lime wedges, if you like.

Preparation time **15 minutes**
Calories per portion **179 Kcal**
Fat per portion **6g**
of which saturated **2.5g**
Serves **4**

Italian-style lunchtime platter

This is a very sociable way to enjoy good food. Italian antipasto is usually soaked in olive oil but this lighter version is so packed with flavour you're guaranteed not to miss it. The platter also makes a good starter to any Italian meal.

Low fat Mozzarella 125g pack, drained
Lean Parma ham 3 thin slices
Artichoke hearts 390g can, drained
Cherry tomatoes 225g (8oz)

Figs 4
Basil leaves a handful
Plain grissini 8
Balsamic vinegar to serve

1 Cut the cheese into 12 sticks. Remove any excess fat from the ham and slice into 12 strips. Carefully wrap a piece of ham around each piece of cheese. Cover and chill until required.

2 Halve the artichoke hearts and cherry tomatoes, and quarter the figs. Arrange on a serving platter. Cover and chill until required.

3 When ready to serve, place the ham and cheese on the platter and sprinkle them with basil leaves. Grind over some black pepper and serve the platter with grissini and balsamic vinegar to dip into or dress the food.

Cook's tip

You can prepare this lunch or starter in advance so you have minimum fuss when your guests arrive. Stand at room temperature for a few minutes before serving to allow the flavours to develop.

Preparation time **10 minutes**
Cooking time **10 minutes**
Calories per portion **289 Kcal**
Fat per portion **18g**
of which saturated **4.8g**
Serves **2**

Eggs Florentine

The word '*Florentine*' is French and refers to the city of Florence in Italy, from where cooks are said to have introduced the French people to spinach. Any dish that is served on a bed of spinach is referred to *à la Florentine*.

Cook's tip

Spinach might look bulky when its fresh, but it wilts and reduces in size very quickly when cooked. Its flavour is intense, which is why some fromage frais stirred into the cooked spinach works so well.

White wine vinegar 2 tsp
Eggs 4
Baby spinach leaves 225g pack
Leek 1 large

Smoked bacon 4 rashers
Low fat natural fromage frais 4 tbsp
Ground nutmeg ¼ tsp

1 Half fill a deep frying pan with water and add the vinegar. Bring to the boil then reduce to a gentle simmer. Carefully break the eggs into the pan and cook for 5–6 minutes (or until cooked to your liking), occasionally spooning the water over the yolks to cook them evenly. Remove from the heat and keep warm in the water until ready to serve.

2 Meanwhile, rinse the spinach and pack into a saucepan without drying. Trim the leek and split lengthwise. Rinse under cold running water to flush out any trapped earth, and then shake well to remove excess water. Shred finely and mix into the spinach. Cover and place over a medium heat for 4–5 minutes until wilted.

3 Preheat the grill to hot and grill the bacon rashers until cooked, turning once.

4 Meanwhile, drain the spinach and leek by pressing against the side of a colander or sieve to remove as much liquid as possible, and return to the saucepan. Stir in the fromage frais and nutmeg and add seasoning to taste.

5 To serve, divide the spinach between two warm serving plates. Drain the eggs using a slotted spoon and place two on top of each pile. Dust with extra nutmeg and black pepper, if liked, and serve immediately with slices of hot toast and grilled smoked bacon.

Preparation time **15 minutes**
Cooking time **5 minutes**
Calories per toastie **275 Kcal**
Fat per toastie **12g**
of which saturated **3.2g**
Makes **1 toastie**

Egg & bacon toastie

If you're wanting a comforting, filling lunch, this combination of bacon and egg can't be beaten. It is readily transportable as a hearty sandwich, too – don't toast the bread and use an extra slice to pop on the top.

Cook's tip

Make into a sandwich by allowing the bacon to cool and cutting into small pieces. Line a piece of bread with leaves and sliced tomato, then top with egg mayonnaise and bacon. Press another piece of bread on top and serve.

Egg 1, hard-boiled
Light mayonnaise 1 tsp
Low fat natural fromage frais 1 tsp
Mustard powder a pinch
Lean unsmoked back bacon 2 rashers, trimmed of any visible fat

Wholemeal bread 1 large slice
Cherry tomatoes 3
Wild rocket leaves or watercress sprigs a handful

1 Peel and mash the egg and mix with the mayonnaise, fromage frais and mustard. Set aside until ready to serve.

2 Preheat the grill to medium/hot and cook the bacon on the grill rack for about 5 minutes, turning halfway through, until golden and crisp. Drain on kitchen paper and keep warm. Toast the bread lightly on each side.

3 To serve, arrange the bacon on the toast and pile the egg on top. Cut each tomato in half and place on top and sprinkle with a few rocket leaves. Season with black pepper and serve immediately.

Vegetarian
VARIETY

Preparation time **10 minutes**
Cooking time **40 minutes**
Calories per portion **394 Kcal**
Fat per portion **17g**
of which saturated **7.5g**
Serves **2**
Suitable for vegetarians

Broccoli & blue cheese soufflé

Quark simply means 'curd' in German and the cheese is said to date from the Iron Age. Quark is made from skimmed milk and is soft and moist, like a cross between yogurt and fromage frais. It is a good source of calcium and low in fat.

Broccoli 1 head, broken into florets and stem sliced
Quark 250g (9oz)
Plain flour 2 tbsp

Mature Stilton 50g (2oz)
Chopped chives 2 tbsp
Eggs 2, separated

1 Preheat the oven to 200°C/400°F/Gas 6. Cook the broccoli in a steamer over a saucepan of boiling water for 12–15 minutes, or until it is tender. Transfer to a saucepan and mash it using a potato masher. Leave it to cool slightly.

2 Beat the quark, plain flour, Stilton, chives and egg yolks into the broccoli. Add seasoning to taste. Whisk the egg whites until they are stiff and then fold them into the broccoli mixture. Divide the mixture between two shallow, round ovenproof dishes, about 12–15cm (5–6in) diameter, doming it up in the centre.

3 Bake the soufflés in the centre of the oven for 20–25 minutes, or until they have just set in the centre. Remove them from the oven and serve immediately with a tomato salad.

Cook's tip

Cook these as soon as you've folded in the whisked egg white, otherwise they will start to lose air. Then serve immediately or they will collapse after being taken out of the oven.

Preparation time **30 minutes**
Cooking time **1 hour**
Calories per portion **216 Kcal**
Fat per portion **8g**
of which saturated **1.9g**
Serves **4**
Suitable for vegetarians + freezing

Broccoli with fresh tomato sauce

Broccoli is a type of cabbage whose flowers have begun to bud but not yet formed. It is exceptionally good for you as it is packed with vitamins and minerals and is recognised as a prime cancer-preventative vegetable.

Cook's tip

For a little extra sharpness, add one or two finely chopped sun-dried tomatoes.

Tomatoes 900g (2lb)
Olive oil 1 tbsp
Onion 1 large, peeled and chopped
Plain flour 1 tbsp
Vegetable stock cube 1, optional

Broccoli 1kg (2lb 3oz), cut into large florets
Cheddar cheese 25–50g (1–2oz), grated
Fresh granary breadcrumbs 25g (1oz)

1 To make the sauce, put the tomatoes into a large heatproof bowl, cover with boiling water and leave to stand for 1–2 minutes or until the skins start to split. Using a slotted spoon, remove the tomatoes from the water and leave to cool.

2 Remove the skin from the tomatoes, and then cut them in half and, using the handle of a small teaspoon, remove the seeds. Roughly chop the tomato flesh.

3 Heat the olive oil in a large saucepan, add the onion and cook gently until softened but not browned, then stir in the flour, crumble in the stock cube (if using) and add the chopped tomatoes.

4 Bring the sauce to the boil, then reduce the heat, partially cover the pan and cook for 30–40 minutes, or until it is reduced and thickened to a coating consistency. Add seasoning to taste.

5 Meanwhile, heat the oven to 220°C/425°F/Gas 7. Steam the broccoli over a saucepan of boiling water for 10 minutes, until just cooked – taking care not to over-cook. Arrange in a large, shallow, ovenproof dish.

6 Pour the tomato sauce over the broccoli. Mix together the cheese and breadcrumbs, sprinkle over the broccoli, and then bake for 25–30 minutes, until piping hot and the cheese mixture is lightly browned. Serve accompanied with granary or wholemeal bread – and a crisp green salad, if wished.

Preparation time **20 minutes**
Cooking time **20 minutes**
Calories per portion **336 Kcal**
Fat per portion **12g**
of which saturated **5.8g**
Serves **4**
Suitable for vegetarians

Asparagus & potato bake

Known as *sparrow grass* in the 18th century, asparagus is a highly regarded vegetable. Its season is relatively short, so buy while you can and enjoy the delicious, woody flavour in this easy meal. The potatoes are steamed to retain more nutrients.

Cook's tip

For added flavour, add a crushed garlic clove to the sauce. Stir it into the melted butter and allow to sauté until soft before adding the flour.

Sweet potatoes 550g (1lb 4oz), peeled and cut into slices about 1cm (½in) thick
New potatoes 450g (1lb) large, scrubbed and cut into slices about 1cm (½in) thick
Asparagus spears 250g (9oz)

Butter 25g (1oz)
Plain flour 25g (1oz)
Vegetable stock cube 1, crumbled
Semi-skimmed milk 450ml (16fl oz)
Mature Cheddar cheese 25–50g (1–2oz), grated

1 Separately, steam the sweet and new potato slices for 15–20 minutes, until just cooked, but taking care not to over cook, as they could break up. Note that the sweet potatoes will cook quicker than the new potatoes

2 Meanwhile, snap off and discard the white, woody end from each of the asparagus spears. Then, wash the spears and cook them in a large saucepan of boiling, lightly salted water for 5–10 minutes (depending on their thickness) until tender.

3 Carefully pour the asparagus into a large colander, refresh under a cold, running tap and drain well. Preheat the oven to 220°C/425°F/Gas 7.

4 When cooked, arrange the new potatoes in the bottom of a large, very lightly oiled, shallow baking dish. Arrange the sweet potatoes on top, and then add the asparagus spears.

5 To make the sauce, melt the butter in a saucepan, stir in the flour, and add the stock cube and milk. Bring to the boil, stirring continuously. Season to taste and pour over the layered vegetables.

6 Sprinkle the cheese over the sauce, and then bake in the oven for 15–20 minutes until bubbling hot, and the cheese is melted and golden brown. Serve with a crisp green salad.

Preparation time **15 minutes**
Cooking time **1¼–1½ hours**
Calories per portion **245 Kcal**
Fat per portion **12g**
of which saturated **4.7g**
Serves **4**
Suitable for vegetarians

Twice-baked potatoes

This comfort food is easy and nutritious. The eggs contain a whole host of vitamins and so provide you with plenty of nutrients essential for the body. Eggs do contain cholesterol but this has much less effect on the level of cholesterol in the blood than saturated fat.

Baking potatoes 2 large
Olive oil 1 tsp
Mature Cheddar cheese 50–75g
(2–3oz), grated

Semi-skimmed milk 1–2 tbsp
Chopped chives 3 tbsp
Eggs 4 large

1 Preheat the oven to 220°C/425°F/Gas 7. Scrub and dry the potatoes, prick them well with a fork, and then brush each one lightly all over with the olive oil.

2 Place the potatoes on a baking tray and bake in the oven for 45 minutes–1 hour, or until they feel soft in the centre when tested with the point of a knife.

3 When cooked, remove the potatoes from the oven and put them onto a board (leaving the oven on). Cut each potato in half lengthways. Then, using a metal spoon, scoop the soft potato out into a bowl, taking care to keep the skins intact. Set the skins aside.

4 Mash the cooked potato well, and then beat in the grated cheese and milk. Season to taste and add the chives.

5 Spoon the potato mixture back into the potato-skin shells. Then, using the back of the metal spoon, make a large, deep hollow in the centre of each potato that is deep enough to take an egg. The potato mixture rises above the edge of the skin, which is important as it prevents the eggs from running out of the hollow.

6 Place the filled potato shells on a baking tray and break the eggs into a teacup, one by one, and very carefully pour into the centre of each potato.

7 Return the potatoes to the oven and cook for 10–15 minutes, until the potato borders are golden brown and the egg whites are set, but the yolks are still soft – taking care not to overcook them.

Cook's tip

For finishing touches, sprinkle a little paprika and extra chopped chives over the potatoes just before serving. These potatoes are delicious served with baked beans.

Preparation time **10 minutes**
Cooking time **1 hour**
Calories per portion **231 Kcal**
Fat per portion **7g**
of which saturated **3.6g**
Serves **2**
Suitable for vegetarians

Baked butternut squash

Squash is a colourful and delicately flavoured vegetable, popular with children. It is rich in carotenoids, which have been shown to protect against cancer and heart disease. Studies have also shown that betacarotene may help to protect the skin from ultra-violet light.

Cook's tip

If the squash skin collapses while you are scraping out the flesh, scrape it all out and pile the mixture into two small, or one larger, gratin dishes for serving – it will taste just as good!

Butternut squash 1
Half fat crème fraîche 3 tbsp
Paprika 1 tsp, plus extra for sprinkling

Spring onions 3, trimmed and finely chopped
Grated Parmesan-like cheese 2 tbsp
Coarse breadcrumbs 2 tbsp

1 Preheat the oven to 200°C/400°F/Gas 6. Halve the squash lengthways and scoop out the seeds and threads with a spoon and discard them. Put on a baking sheet and roast for 40–50 minutes until the flesh is soft when you test it with a knife.

2 Put the squash halves on a board and leave until cool enough to handle (or put on thick rubber gloves to hold the hot vegetable and do it straightaway). Scrape the flesh into a bowl, leaving a thin border and keeping the skin and shape of the squash intact.

3 Roughly mash the flesh with a fork and mix in the crème fraîche, paprika and spring onions.

4 Pile the mixture back into the shells. Put on a baking tray and sprinkle with the grated cheese and breadcrumbs and a little more paprika. Put the squash shells back in the oven and cook for another 10–15 minutes until browned on top and piping hot.

Preparation time **10 minutes**
Cooking time **40 minutes**
Calories per portion **389 Kcal**
Fat per portion **26g**
of which saturated **11.4g**
Serves **4**
Suitable for vegetarians + freezing

Vegetable crunch

This dish really is full of goodness. The vegetables and tomatoes are full of vitamins and minerals and the nuts and cheese contain calcium and magnesium. With so much variety packed into this dish you will be well ahead with your five servings a day (see page 6).

Cook's tip

Try this recipe with other vegetables, such as courgettes and peppers, and a different type of nut, like hazelnuts.

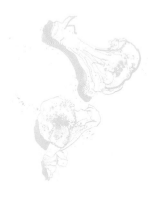

Spray oil a few bursts
Onion 1, peeled and sliced
Tomato purée 2 tbsp
Broccoli 225g (8oz), broken into small florets
Carrots 225g (8oz), peeled and thinly sliced
Mushrooms 175g (6oz), wiped and sliced

Chopped tomatoes 400g can
Chopped parsley 1 tbsp
Mixed dried herbs ½ tsp
Blanched almonds 50g (2oz)
Butter 50g (2oz)
Wholemeal flour 75g (3oz)
Rolled oats 25g (1oz)
Cheddar cheese 75g (3oz), grated

1 Preheat the oven to 200°C/400°F/Gas 6. Spray a saucepan with oil and add the onion. Cook until it has softened.

2 Add the tomato pureé and the remaining vegetables and herbs and cook gently for 10 minutes, until the vegetables are tender. Add the nuts and then season to taste and spoon the mixture into a shallow ovenproof dish.

3 Rub the butter into the flour until the mixture resembles fine breadcrumbs. Stir in the rolled oats and cheese.

4 Spoon the crumble mixture over the vegetables and then bake for 30 minutes until browned. Serve with green leaf and herb salad.

Preparation time **10 minutes**
Cooking time **40 minutes**
Calories per portion **195 Kcal**
Fat per portion **4g**
of which saturated **0.6g**
Serves **4**
Suitable for vegetarians

Lentil moussaka

Lentils are one of the best sources of vegetarian protein available. They contain potassium, zinc and folic acid. They also help to regulate digestive function. Try using them in this wholesome dish, which is perfect for a cold British, blustery evening.

Cook's tip

This recipe may be made up and assembled in the ovenproof dish up to 24 hours in advance, and then kept chilled in the fridge. If it's been chilled then allow extra time for it to cook in the oven.

Chopped tomatoes 227g can
Vegetable stock 300ml (½ pint)
Puy lentils 110g (4oz)
Onion 1, peeled and sliced
Garlic 2 cloves, peeled and sliced
Button mushrooms 250g (9oz), wiped and sliced
Celery 2 sticks, chopped

Aubergines 2, sliced
Olive oil spray a few bursts
Chopped oregano 1 tbsp
Ground cinnamon ½ tsp
Grated nutmeg ½ tsp
Tomatoes 3, sliced
Quark 125g (4½oz)
Egg 1

1 Preheat the oven to 200°C/400°F/Gas 6 and also preheat the grill to hot. Tip the chopped tomatoes into a saucepan and add the vegetable stock, lentils, onion, garlic, mushrooms and celery. Bring the mixture to the boil, then reduce the heat and simmer for 20 minutes until the lentils are just tender and most of the liquid has been absorbed.

2 Meanwhile, spread out the aubergine slices on a baking sheet. Spray the slices with 2 bursts of olive oil spray. Place under the grill and cook for 3–4 minutes, until the slices start to turn golden, then turn over, spray with another 2 bursts oil and return to the grill for a further 3–4 minutes until golden.

3 Stir the oregano, cinnamon and nutmeg into the lentils and season to taste. Spoon half of the mixture into a deep ovenproof dish. Spread half of the tomatoes over the lentils and then add half the aubergine slices, overlapping them slightly. Spoon over the remaining lentil mixture, and then cover with the remaining tomatoes and aubergine.

4 Beat together the quark and egg. Spread over the aubergines. Bake the moussaka in the centre of the oven for 15–20 minutes, or until the topping is golden. Serve immediately.

Preparation time **30 minutes**
Cooking time **45 minutes**
Calories per portion **280 Kcal**
Fat per portion **2g**
of which saturated **0.3g**
Serves **4**
Suitable for vegetarians

Vegetable & barley bake

Barley is the oldest cultivated cereal in Europe and possibly the world. Pearl barley has been ground to remove the outer husk of the bran. However, it is still a good source of fibre and also contains potassium and other minerals to benefit your body.

Cook's tip

Ring the changes by replacing the carrots with a red pepper and the celery with 2 tomatoes.

Dried wild mushrooms 25g (1oz)
Spray oil a few bursts
Onion 1 large, peeled and diced
Garlic 2 cloves, peeled and chopped
Celery 2 sticks, chopped

Button mushrooms 110g (4oz), wiped
Carrots 2, peeled and diced
Pearl barley 250g (9oz), rinsed
Vegetable stock 300ml (½ pint)
Mixed dried herbs 1 tsp

1 Preheat the oven to 180°C/350°F/Gas 4. Soak the dried mushrooms in 300ml (½ pint) hot water for 30 minutes.

2 Meanwhile, spray a large pan with oil and sauté the onion, garlic and celery for 6 minutes. Add the button mushrooms and carrots and cook for a further 5 minutes.

3 When the soaking time has elapsed, drain the mushrooms, reserving the liquid, and rinse thoroughly.

4 Add the barley, stock, herbs, rinsed wild mushrooms and their liquid and bring to the boil. Transfer to an ovenproof dish, cover and cook in the oven for 15 minutes or until the barley is tender. Stir and add extra water if it looks too dry. Return to the oven and cook for another 12 minutes.

Preparation time **5 minutes**
Cooking time **25 minutes**
Calories per portion **249 Kcal**
Fat per portion **3g**
of which saturated **0.9g**
Serves **4**
Suitable for vegetarians

Vegetable curry

A scrumptiously spicy dish, which is easy to prepare and ideal for vegetarians. The carrots are an excellent source of beta-carotene, which our bodies turn into vitamin A. Beta-carotene also acts as an antioxidant, protecting cell membranes.

Cook's tip

If you want to serve with raita, simply mix some chopped mint and cucumber with low fat natural yogurt.

Spray oil a few bursts
Onion 1, peeled and chopped
Curry powder 1 tbsp
Paprika 1 tsp
Tomato purée 2 tsp
Lemon juice 2 tsp
Apricot jam or redcurrant jelly 1 tbsp

Semi-skimmed milk 300ml (½ pint)
Raisins or sultanas 50g (2oz)
Carrots 400g (14oz), peeled and sliced
Cauliflower 400g (14oz), broken into florets
Potatoes 400g (14oz), peeled and cubed

1 Spray a large pan with oil and add the onion. Fry gently for a few minutes, without browning. Add the curry powder and paprika and cook for a further 2–3 minutes.

2 Add the tomato purée, lemon juice, jam or jelly, milk and raisins or sultanas. Bring to the boil and then simmer, uncovered, for 10 minutes.

3 Meanwhile, cook the vegetables in a pan of boiling water for 5–10 minutes, until tender, adding shredded green cauliflower leaves, if any, for the last 2 minutes.

4 Drain the vegetables and stir them into the curry sauce. Simmer until all vegetables are tender, topping up with extra milk if sauce boils dry. Serve the curry with basmati or brown rice.

Preparation time **15 minutes**
Cooking time **10 minutes**
Calories per portion **255 Kcal**
Fat per portion **5g**
of which saturated **0.6g**
Serves **4**
Suitable for vegetarians

Pancakes with vegetables & tofu

These oriental pancakes are full of health-boosting ingredients, providing you with essential minerals, such as potassium, which is needed to regulate the body's metabolism. Ginger is an excellent anti-inflammatory.

Cook's tip

Chinese pancakes are available from Chinese shops and supermarkets nationwide. If you cannot obtain Chinese panckes, soft flour tortillas taste just as good.

Vegetable oil 2 tsp
Garlic 1 clove, peeled and chopped
Root ginger 2.5cm (1in) piece, peeled and cut into thin strips
Spring onions 1 bunch, trimmed and sliced
Mangetout 110g (4oz), trimmed and thinly sliced lengthways
Baby corn 110g (4oz), trimmed and cut in half lengthwise

Tofu 225g (8oz), drained and cut into 12 x 1cm (½in) pieces
Reduced salt soy sauce 1 tbsp
Hoisin sauce 1 tbsp
Beanshoots 75g (3oz)
Chives 1 small bunch, optional
Chinese pancakes 12 soft or **soft tortillas** 4
Chinese leaves ¼ head
Sweet chilli sauce to serve

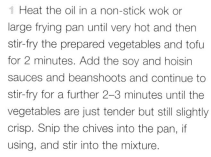

1 Heat the oil in a non-stick wok or large frying pan until very hot and then stir-fry the prepared vegetables and tofu for 2 minutes. Add the soy and hoisin sauces and beanshoots and continue to stir-fry for a further 2–3 minutes until the vegetables are just tender but still slightly crisp. Snip the chives into the pan, if using, and stir into the mixture.

2 Meanwhile, heat the pancakes or tortillas according to the packet instructions and keep warm until ready to serve. Shred the Chinese leaves finely.

3 To serve, divide the vegetable and tofu mixture between the pancakes or tortillas and roll up with some shredded Chinese leaves. Serve with sweet chilli sauce to dip.

Preparation time **5 minutes**
Cooking time **45 minutes**
Calories per portion **220 Kcal**
Fat per portion **6g**
of which saturated **1.8g**
Serves **2**
Suitable for vegetarians + freezing

Vegetable popovers

A great vegetarian alternative to toad-in-the-hole, these popovers are a fast and fun way to enjoy vegetables. The preparation time is wonderfully brief, so you can pop them in the oven and then put up your feet while they are cooking.

Cook's tip

If you cook the mixture in a non-stick tin (any shape), then you won't need to use the 4 bursts of oil for greasing the tin as they will just pop out.

Red pepper 1, deseeded and sliced
Button mushrooms 110g (4oz), wiped and halved
Red onion 1, peeled and sliced
Olive oil spray 6 bursts

Egg 1
Semi-skimmed milk 150ml (¼ pint)
Plain flour 50g (2oz)
Chopped thyme 1 tbsp

1 Preheat the oven to 220°C/425°F/Gas 7. Spread out the red pepper, mushrooms and red onion on a baking tray and spray with 2 bursts of olive oil. Place the tray towards the top of the oven and cook the vegetables for 20–25 minutes, turning them occasionally, until they start to turn golden.

2 Meanwhile, make the batter by whisking together the egg, milk and flour and then stirring in the thyme.

3 Spray a burst of olive oil into each cavity of a four-hole Yorkshire pudding tin to grease them. Divide the vegetables between the cavities in the tin and place the tin in the oven for 2–3 minutes, to heat.

4 Remove the tin from the oven, immediately pour the batter over the vegetables and cook for a further 20–25 minutes, or until the batter has risen and has set.

5 Remove the tin from the oven and use a palette knife to lift the popovers and transfer onto plates. Serve with baked beans and steamed broccoli.

Preparation time **20 minutes**
Cooking time **10–12 minutes**
Calories per portion **416 Kcal**
Fat per portion **13g**
of which saturated **3.3g**
Serves **2**
Suitable for vegetarians

Pasta primavera

In Italian, 'primavera' translates roughly as 'in the spring style'. This pasta dish includes nutritious spring vegetables and herbs to pep up the subtle flavour of the linguini – they add lots of vibrant colour, too.

Tomatoes 2 large
Courgettes 2 large
Carrots 2 large, peeled
Spring onions 4 large, trimmed
Olive oil 1 tsp and 1 tbsp

Pasta, e.g. linguini 110–150g (4–5oz)
Chopped parsley 4–6 tbsp
Basil leaves a handful, finely shredded
Parmesan-like cheese 20g (¾oz), grated

1 Put the tomatoes into a large heatproof bowl, cover with boiling water and leave to stand for 1–2 minutes or until the skins start to split. Using a slotted spoon, remove the tomatoes from the water, place on a board, and leave them to cool for 3–4 minutes or until they are cool enough to handle.

2 Remove the skin from the tomatoes, cut them in half and then, using the handle of a small teaspoon, remove the seeds. Chop the tomato flesh into small squares.

3 Cut the ends off the courgettes and use a vegetable peeler to cut the courgettes and carrots into thin ribbon strips – pulling the peeler from one end to the other. Cut the spring onions in half lengthways, and then into thin strips lengthways.

4 Bring a large saucepan of water to the boil. Add the teaspoon of olive oil, then add the pasta and cook according to the packet's instructions. Meanwhile, put the courgette, carrot and spring onion strips into a steamer and steam for 10–12 minutes, until they are cooked but still slightly crisp.

5 Heat the tablespoon of olive oil in a saucepan, add the diced tomatoes and cook them until very hot, taking care not to let them soften too much or break up. Add the drained pasta, steamed vegetables, parsley and basil to the tomatoes, toss gently together and serve immediately, sprinkled with cheese and freshly ground black pepper to taste.

Preparation time **20 minutes**
Cooking time **1 hour**
Calories per portion **170 Kcal**
Fat per portion **3g**
of which saturated **1.2g**
Serves **6**
Suitable for vegetarians + freezing

Leeks & roots lasagne

This colourful mixture of root vegetables will release energy slowly so should fill you up for longer and give you a fair portion of fibre, too. Sweet potatoes and tomatoes are especially high in vitamins A and C, crucial for good skin.

Cook's tip

Fresh egg lasagne comes in 300g packs or 12 sheets. Freeze the rest of the sheets for use another time.

Olive oil 1 tsp
Onion 1, peeled and diced
Carrots 2, peeled and diced
Sweet potato 1, peeled and diced
Parsnip 1, peeled and diced
Celery 2 sticks, chopped
Garlic 2 cloves, peeled and chopped

White wine 3 tbsp
Thyme sprigs 2
Plum tomatoes 2 x 400g cans
Leeks 2, trimmed and thinly sliced
Fresh egg lasagne 4–5 sheets
Gruyère/Cheddar cheese 25g (1oz), grated

1 Heat the olive oil in a large pan over a medium heat and add the onion, carrots, sweet potato, parsnip and celery as you prepare them. Cook, covered, stirring every so often, for 10 minutes until the vegetables are just tender. Add the garlic, wine, thyme sprigs and tomatoes and simmer, half-covered, for 15 minutes until the sauce thickens. Season to taste.

2 Meanwhile, blanch the leeks in a pan of boiling water for 5 minutes. Put the lasagne sheets into a lasagne dish. Drain the leeks over the dish so the water helps to soften the sheets (or use boiling water from the kettle) and leave for 5 minutes. Cool the leeks under cold running water to keep their colour, then leave to drain.

3 Preheat the oven to 200°C/400°F/Gas 6. Take the lasagne sheets out of the dish and discard the water.

4 Spoon half the tomato sauce into the lasagne dish. Place 2 sheets of lasagne on top. Spoon in almost all the sauce, keeping back 2 spoonfuls, and cover with the other 2 sheets of lasagne. Fill the gaps with the remaining sheet.

5 Spread the leeks over the lasagne and spoon the remaining tomato sauce on top. Sprinkle with the grated cheese. Bake for 25 minutes until golden brown. Serve hot with green beans.

Preparation time **20 minutes**
Cooking time **25 minutes**
Calories per portion **464 Kcal**
Fat per portion **11g**
of which saturated **4.3g**
Serves **4**
Suitable for vegetarians

Creamy Quorn & macaroni bake

The unique ingredient in all Quorn foods is mycoprotein, a nutritious member of the fungi family. Mycoprotein is an excellent source of protein and also contains fibre, helping to maintain a healthy digestive system. This dish also provides you with calcium.

Cook's tip

Replace the asparagus with small broccoli florets or pieces of chopped courgette if preferred.

Asparagus spears 225g (8oz), woody ends trimmed
Leek 1 large
Macaroni 225g (8oz)
Quorn sausages 250g pack
Spray oil a few bursts

Cherry tomatoes 110g (4oz)
Cornflour 2 tbsp
Semi-skimmed milk 600ml (1 pint)
Light soft cream cheese 100g (3½oz)
Wholemeal breadcrumbs 50g (2oz)
Grated Parmesan-like cheese 1 tbsp

1 Cut the asparagus spears into 2.5cm (1in) lengths and place in a steamer. Trim the leek and split lengthwise. Rinse under cold running water to flush out any trapped earth, and then shake well to remove excess water. Shred finely and place on top of the asparagus and cover with a lid. Bring a saucepan of water to the boil.

2 Add the macaroni to the pan and cook as per the packet's instructions. Place the covered steamer over the macaroni for 10 minutes of the cooking time, until the vegetables are tender. Drain the macaroni, return to the pan and add the vegetables.

3 Meanwhile, cut each sausage into four diagonal slices. Spray a non-stick frying pan lightly with spray oil and heat until hot. Stir-fry the sausage pieces for about 5 minutes until golden all over. Drain on kitchen paper. Halve the cherry tomatoes and toss into the vegetable macaroni along with the sausage pieces. Cover and set aside.

4 Place the cornflour in a saucepan and blend with a little of the milk to form a smooth paste. Stir in the remaining milk and heat gently, stirring, until boiling. Cook for 1 minute until thickened. Remove from the heat, season to taste and stir in the soft cheese and then mix into the vegetables and macaroni.

5 Preheat the grill to hot. Transfer the macaroni mix to a shallow heatproof dish and sprinkle the breadcrumbs and cheese over the top. Cook under the grill for 2–3 minutes until golden and crisp. Serve with green salad.

Preparation time **15 minutes**
Cooking time **55 minutes**
Calories per portion **384 Kcal**
Fat per portion **6g**
of which saturated **1g**
Serves **4**
Suitable for vegetarians + freezing

Chilli con Quorn cottage pie

A lower fat version of a traditional cottage pie, this dish includes the addition of chilli to give it a bit of a kick. The kidney beans are an excellent provider of vegetable protein and also help to lower cholesterol.

Cook's tip

For a more traditional vegetarian cottage pie, omit the spices and kidney beans. You could include some mushrooms along with the onion in step 2.

Potatoes 900g (2lb), peeled and cut into small pieces
Egg 1, beaten
Low fat natural fromage frais 4 tbsp
Chopped parsley 4 tbsp
Onion 1 large, peeled and chopped
Vegetable stock 300ml (½ pint)

Quorn mince 350g (12oz)
Chopped tomatoes with garlic 400g can
Hot chilli powder ½–1 tsp
Ground cumin ½–1 tsp
Kidney beans 410g can, drained and rinsed

1 Preheat the oven to 200°C/400°F/Gas 6. Place the potato pieces in a large saucepan. Cover with water and bring to the boil; cook for about 10 minutes until tender. Drain well and return to the saucepan. Add half the beaten egg and mash well using a potato masher or fork and stir in the fromage frais and parsley and season to taste. Set aside.

2 Place the onion in a saucepan. Pour over half the stock, bring to the boil, cover and simmer for 5 minutes until tender. Stir in the remaining stock, Quorn, chopped tomatoes, chilli powder to taste, cumin and kidney beans. Bring to the boil, cover and simmer for 5 minutes. Season to taste.

3 Transfer the Quorn chilli mixture to an ovenproof dish and pile the mashed potato on top, making sure the vegetables are completely covered. Stand on a baking sheet (in case of spillage during cooking), brush with the remaining egg and bake in the oven for 30–35 minutes until golden. Serve immediately while piping hot.

Fabulous
FISH

Preparation time **5 minutes**
Cooking time **20 minutes**
Calories per portion **234 Kcal**
Fat per portion **8g**
of which saturated **1g**
Serves **2**
Suitable for freezing

Fish Provençal

Provence is well known for its olives and other Mediterranean foods and here these Provençal flavours are combined to create a delicious fish dish which is superbly easy to make. Make the most of any special offers on white fish – most types will be suitable.

Cook's tip

For really succulent fish, instead of grilling, poach in a pan of gently simmering water for around 5 minutes, turning halfway through if it is not entirely submerged.

Spray oil a few bursts
Onion 1 large, peeled and chopped
Garlic 2 cloves, peeled and crushed
Chopped tomatoes 400g can, drained

Olives 50g (2oz), pitted
Thyme 2 tbsp
Cod, coley or haddock steaks 2 x 150g (5oz)

1 Preheat the grill to medium. Spray a large frying pan with oil and gently fry the onion for around 5 minutes, until soft. Add the garlic, tomatoes, olives and thyme and bring to the boil. Season to taste and simmer for 10 minutes.

2 Meanwhile, grill the fish for 4 minutes on each side. Then place the fish in the frying pan and coat with the sauce. Serve immediately on individual plates with new potatoes and a rocket salad.

Preparation time **5 minutes**
Cooking time **15 minutes**
Calories per portion **142 Kcal**
Fat per portion **2g**
of which saturated **0.3g**
Serves **2**

Crusted cod

Avoid the fish and chip shop with this healthy alternative. Serve with cheat's chips (see cook's tip) and plenty of plump petit pois. White fish is a very low fat form of protein and is delicious served with this crunchy topping.

Cook's tip

For cheat's chips; cook two small baking potatoes in the microwave, on high, for 5 minutes. Cut into chunky chips, place on a baking tray and spray with oil. Bake in the oven alongside the fish.

Cod filets 2
Chopped parsley 2 tbsp
Lemon 1, grated zest

Wholemeal breadcrumbs 25g (1oz)
Spray oil 2–3 bursts

1 Preheat the oven to 200°C/400°F/Gas 6. Place the cod fillets, skin-side down, on a sheet of baking parchment on a baking tray.

2 Mix the parsley and lemon zest into the breadcrumbs and season to taste. Press the mixture on top of the cod. Spray the topping with the olive oil spray.

3 Roast the fish towards the top of the oven for 15–20 minutes, or until the topping is a light golden colour, and the fish feels tender when pierced with a thin knife. Serve immediately, accompanied with chips and peas.

Preparation time **20 minutes**
Cooking time **6–8 minutes**
Calories per kebab **247 Kcal**
Fat per kebab **4g**
of which saturated **1.2g**
Makes **4 kebabs**

Fish kebabs with spinach salad

Spinach is an excellent source of iron and other minerals. It helps to boost the immune system and works as a natural antioxidant. Here it is combined with onion and sesame seeds, a good source of selenium, for a scrumptious salad, served with healthy seafood.

Cook's tip

For a crunchy texture, replace the sesame seeds with pumpkin seeds in the spinach salad.

Tomato ketchup 2 tbsp
Reduced salt soy sauce 1 tbsp
Chilli powder ½ tsp
Large, cooked, peeled tiger prawn tails 20, rinsed and dried
Lemon sole fillets 2 x 350g packets

Lime slices 8
Lemon slices 8
Baby spinach leaves 225g pack
Red onion 1 small, peeled, thinly sliced
Sesame seeds 1–2 tsp, toasted
Seasoned rice vinegar 1–2 tsp

1 In a large bowl, mix together the tomato ketchup, soy sauce and chilli powder for the marinade. Add the prawns and coat evenly. Cover and leave for 5–10 minutes. Wash the sole fillets in cold water, cut them in half lenghways and dry carefully on kitchen paper.

2 To assemble the skewers, first place a sole fillet skinned-side up on a board and with the head end nearest to you. Place a marinated prawn at the head end, with its curved side towards you and the tail slightly overhanging the edge. Take another prawn and place it with the curved side away from you and fitting closely with the first prawn. Tightly roll up the fillet and thread onto a skewer, ensuring you pass the skewer through the prawns. Place a slice of lime on a slice of lemon, and thread onto the skewer.

3 Repeat with another fillet and citrus slices and then thread one of the remaining prawns onto the end. Repeat on three more skewers.

4 Place the remaining ingredients into a bowl, toss gently together and set aside.

5 Heat the grill to moderately high and line the grill pan with non-stick baking foil. Place the kebabs in the pan, brush with any remaining marinade and cook for 6–8 minutes, turning once, until the sole fillets are cooked through and the prawns are piping hot. Serve immediately, accompanied with the spinach salad and fresh granary bread.

Preparation time **10 minutes**
Cooking time **15 minutes**
Calories per parcel **87 Kcal**
Fat per parcel **1g**
of which saturated **0.2g**
Makes **4 parcels**
Suitable for freezing

Monkfish cabbage parcels

Monkfish seems to have adopted various names in different parts of the UK. In Scotland, it is referred to as 'Molly Gowan' and in Ireland, as 'Frogfish', which would make sense given its frog-like appearance. Its tail is the only part that is usually eaten and it is delicous!

Cook's tip

Take care not to overcook the cabbage leaves or they will go soggy – running them under the cold water once cooked will cool them quickly and help to preserve the green colour.

Savoy cabbage 4 large leaves
Plum tomatoes 2, peeled, deseeded and chopped

Chopped basil leaves 1 tbsp
Monkfish tail 450g (1lb), cleaned

1 Bring a large pan of water to the boil. Plunge the cabbage leaves into the water and cook them for about 30 seconds, until they have softened, then drain and rinse under cold running water.

2 Mix together the chopped tomatoes and basil and add seasoning to taste.

3 Cut out any thick stems from the cabbage leaves and then lay the leaves out on the worksurface, overlapping them so that they are slightly longer than the length of monkfish tail.

4 Cut the monkfish in half and remove the central bone. Lay the 2 pieces of filleted fish side by side on the cabbage leaves, and spread the tomato mixture between them. Fold in the ends of the cabbage, and then roll the cabbage leaves around the fish to totally cover it. Tie the parcel with string to help retain its shape.

5 Place the cabbage-wrapped monkfish in a steamer over hot water, and steam it for about 15 minutes, or until the fish feels tender when pierced with a fine skewer. Remove the parcels from the steamer, cut off the string and serve with steamed new potatoes, asparagus spears and carrots.

Preparation time **10 minutes plus**
30 minutes marinating
Cooking time **15 minutes**
Calories per portion **296 Kcal**
Fat per portion **21g**
of which saturated **4g**
Serves **4**

Spiced mackerel

Bursting with omega 3, which can help reduce arthritis inflammation, fresh mackerel are in abundance during the summer months, so take advantage of them and give them a subtle Indian flavour with this tasty recipe.

Cook's tip

Use a good pair of tweezers to remove the bones. It's a bit tedious, but necessary if you have fussy fish eaters.

Mackerel fillets 8 small
Low fat natural yogurt 2 tbsp
Lemon juice 2 tbsp
Root ginger 1cm (½in) piece, peeled and grated

Cayenne pepper 2 tsp
Ground cumin 2 tsp
Garam masala 2 tsp
Spray oil a few bursts

1 Rinse the mackerel fillets under cold running water. Pat them dry on kitchen paper. Remove the inevitable bones if you prefer. Slash the skin of each fillet with three diagonal cuts.

2 In a large shallow bowl, mix together the yogurt, lemon juice, ginger, spices and add black pepper. Add the fish and, using your hands, gently rub the marinade all over them. Cover and leave in a cool place – not the fridge – for 30 minutes.

3 Heat a griddle pan, preferably non-stick, over a medium heat. Take 4 fish fillets out of the marinade, easing off the mixture with a knife or your fingers. Lightly spray each fish with oil. Add a light sprinkling of salt and cook them, skin-side up, for 3 minutes; flip them over and cook for another 2 minutes. Set aside in a warm oven and cook the other 4 fillets in the same way. Serve on a bed of couscous and vegetables with lemon wedges, and green leaves.

Preparation time **10 minutes**
Cooking time **45 minutes**
Calories per portion **535 Kcal**
Fat per portion **26g**
of which saturated **6.1g**
Serves **4**

Smoked fish kedgeree

Traditionally eaten at breakfast time, kedgeree can also be eaten as a light supper dish, accompanied with a green salad. This healthy version uses less rice combined with a higher proportion of fish, which is high in protein and essential fats.

Cook's tip

Saffron was traditionally used to turn rice a bright yellow, but turmeric is a cheaper alternative. It is used in many curries, too.

Un-dyed smoked haddock fillet 680g (1½lb)
Olive oil ½ tbsp
Red onion 1–2 large, peeled, halved and cut into thick wedges
Long grain rice 110g (4oz)
Turmeric a pinch

Smoked, peppered mackerel fillets 250g (9oz)
Eggs 2 large, hard-boiled, shelled and chopped
Watercress 85g (3½oz), roughly chopped
Lemon wedges to serve, optional

1 Wash the haddock under a cold, running tap and put into a large lidded frying pan, cutting the fish into two pieces to fit. Barely cover the haddock with cold water and bring to the boil. Turn off the heat, cover with the lid and leave the haddock to stand for 10–15 minutes, during which time it will cook through completely.

2 Drain the haddock (reserving the liquid), then remove the skin, flake the flesh and remove any bones. Cover the flakes and set aside while you prepare the rice. Wash and dry the frying pan.

3 Heat the olive oil in the frying pan, then add the onion wedges and cook them gently until just beginning to soften. Stir the rice into the onion, add 300ml (½ pint) of the reserved liquid and turmeric and bring to the boil. Then reduce the heat, cover the pan and cook gently for 20–25 minutes, until the rice is cooked.

4 Meanwhile, flake and bone the mackerel fillets.

5 When the rice is cooked, gently mix in the haddock and mackerel and heat through until piping hot.

6 Using a fork, gently mix both the egg and watercress into the kedgeree and serve immediately with lemon wedges, if using.

Preparation time **15 minutes**
Cooking time **10 minutes**
Calories per portion **185 Kcal**
Fat per portion **8g**
of which saturated **1.6g**
Serves **4**

Tuna steak with salsa verde

Fresh tuna is much more widely available these days, which is good news as it contains much more omega 3 than canned tuna, while being much lower in fat than tuna in oil. The salsa gives the tuna a zingy vibrancy, ideal for a quick summer meal.

Cook's tip

Fresh tuna is best if it is just cooked on the outside and pink in the middle; so try not to overcook as it becomes dry and tough.

Tuna steaks 4 x 110g (4oz)
Olive oil 4 tsp
Lemon 1, grated zest and strained juice
Good pinch of sugar
Garlic 1 clove, peeled and finely chopped
Baby gherkins (cornichons) 4, finely chopped

Capers 1 tbsp, rinsed and chopped if large
Anchovy fillets 4, chopped, optional
Chopped parsley 3 tbsp
Chopped mint leaves 2 tbsp
Chopped basil leaves 2 tbsp

1 Put the tuna steaks in a large shallow dish with 2 teaspoons of the olive oil, half the lemon zest and half the lemon juice. Coat the tuna well and leave to marinade while you make the salsa.

2 To make the salsa, in a bowl mix the rest of the oil, lemon zest and 1–2 tablespoons of the lemon juice with the sugar, garlic, gherkins, capers, anchovies (if using) and chopped herbs.

3 Heat a griddle pan or frying pan (preferably non-stick) until hot. Cook the tuna steaks, 2 at time for 2–3 minutes each side.

4 Serve each steak with a spoonful of salsa on top. Accompany with new potatoes and rocket salad.

Preparation time **5 minutes plus 1 hour marinating**
Cooking time **15 minutes**
Calories per portion **167 Kcal**
Fat per portion **5g**
of which saturated **1.2g**
Serves **2**

Teriyaki griddled tuna

'*Teriyaki*' is a Japanese term that refers to a special glaze applied to food; '*teri*' means gloss and '*yaki*' refers to grilling or frying. The sauce is a combination of sake, soy sauce and mirin, and adds a lovely flavour to the tuna in this dish.

Cook's tip

Soy sauce can be used as a substitute for teriyaki sauce if you're unable to find it.

Teriyaki sauce 2 tbsp
Garlic 1 clove, peeled and crushed
Root ginger 1cm (½in) piece, peeled and grated

Tuna steaks 2 x 110g (4oz)
Spring onions 4, trimmed and cut into strips
Spray oil a few bursts

1 Mix together the teriyaki sauce, garlic and ginger in a shallow dish and add the tuna and spring onions. Cover the dish and leave to marinade for at least 1 hour, or overnight for a stronger flavour.

2 Heat a ridged frying pan and spray lightly with oil. Add the tuna and spring onions to the pan. Cook the tuna for 3–4 minutes on each side until it is just turning golden and is almost, but not completely, cooked through. Turn the spring onions regularly so that they wilt.

3 Remove the tuna from the pan and scatter 2 spring onions over each portion and serve with a fresh green salad, or Lime-dressed courgettes on page 155.

Preparation time **20 minutes**
Cooking time **10 minutes**
Calories per triangle **223 Kcal**
Fat per triangle **14g**
of which saturated **7.4g**
Makes **8 triangles**

Salmon & cheese triangles

Filo pastry contains less fat than other types of pastry and works really well with salmon. The calcium found in the Wensleydale and soft cream cheese helps to build and maintain strong bones and teeth.

Cook's tip

Some packs of filo pastry contain 6 sheets of filo. If this is the case, use the same amount of filling but make 6 slightly more generously filled triangles.

Light soft cream cheese 110g (4oz)
Wensleydale cheese 110g (4oz), grated
Salmon 200g can, drained and flaked

Lemon juice 1 tsp
Chopped parsley 1 tbsp
Filo pastry 8 sheets
Unsalted butter 50g (2oz), melted

1 Preheat the oven to 200°C/400°F/Gas 6. In a bowl, mix together the cheeses, salmon, lemon juice and parsley.

2 Brush a sheet of filo pastry with a little butter and then fold in half lengthways and position it so that the short sides are at the top and bottom. Brush with more butter and place a spoonful of filling at the bottom end and to the left-hand side of the strip, nearest to you. Lift the right-hand corner of the pastry up and over the filling to form a triangle. Then, fold the triangle directly up and over the next part of the filo.

3 Lift the left-hand corner and fold it over to the right – forming another triangle. Fold the triangle directly up again. Repeat the folding until the filling is completely encased in the pastry strip.

4 Repeat with the remaining sheets of pastry and filling. Place on a greased baking sheet and brush with the remaining melted butter.

5 Bake in the oven for 10 minutes until they are golden brown. Serve hot with roasted vegetables.

Preparation time **20 minutes**
Cooking time **15 minutes**
Calories per portion **272 Kcal**
Fat per portion **13g**
of which saturated **2.5g**
Serves **4**

Five-spice salmon

Salmon is a rich source of heart healthy omega-3 fatty acids. The salmon is dusted in five-spice powder, which is a very fragrant and delicate seasoning made from ground star anise, fennel, cinnamon, cloves and Szechuan pepper.

Skinless salmon fillets 4 x 110g (4oz)
Five-spice powder 2 tsp
Large leek 1, trimmed
Large carrots 2, trimmed and peeled
Celeriac 450g (1lb), peeled
Lemon juice 2 tbsp

Spray oil a few bursts
Root ginger 2.5cm (1in) piece, peeled and cut into thin strips
Sweet sherry 2 tbsp
Reduced salt soy sauce 1 tbsp
Shredded spring onions to garnish

1 Wash and pat dry the salmon. Dust both sides of the fish with the five-spice powder and set aside.

2 Next prepare the vegetables. Split the leek lengthwise. Rinse under cold running water to flush out any trapped earth, and then shake well to remove excess water. Cut into long thin slices. Cut the carrots and celeriac into fine matchstick-like slices or grate coarsely. Toss in the lemon juice.

3 Lightly spray a large non-stick frying pan and heat until hot. Press the salmon into the pan to seal for 1 minute, then reduce the heat and cook for 5–6 minutes. Turn over and cook for a further 5 minutes or until cooked through. Drain and keep warm.

4 Meanwhile, lightly spray a non-stick wok or large frying pan and heat until hot. Add the prepared vegetables, ginger, sherry and soy sauce and stir-fry for 4–5 minutes until just beginning to wilt.

5 To serve, spoon the vegetables onto hot serving plates and top with a piece of salmon. Garnish with a little shredded spring onion.

Cook's tip

If you are unable to obtain celeriac for this recipe, simply replace with 2 chopped celery sticks and an extra carrot cut into thin strips.

Preparation time **1 hour plus**
1–2 hours chilling
Cooking time **15 minutes**
Calories per sushi **35 Kcal**
Fat per sushi **1g**
of which saturated **0.1g**
Makes **40 sushi**

Ginger sushi

Making sushi does require both time and patience, but the end result is worth every minute. Ingredients and equipment for making sushi can now be found easily in most supermarkets, and, of course, in oriental outlets. Sushi make impressive canapés or a light supper dish.

Cook's tip

Although the preparation of sushi may seem complicated at first, when you have made it once you will find it much easier and quicker the next time. It is worth buying a bamboo rolling mat (available at most supermarkets) to help with the process.

Sushi rice 250g (9oz)
Large red pepper 1
Large green pepper 1
Frozen, cooked, peeled king prawns 220g bag, thawed and well drained
Lemon 1, grated zest and 2 tbsp juice
Tabasco sauce 2–3 drops
Seasoned rice vinegar 4 tbsp

Wasabi paste ½–1 tsp
Sushi nori 11g pack (5 sheets)
Finely chopped stem ginger 1 tsp
Spring onions 2 large, trimmed and cut lengthways into thin strips
Smoked salmon 110g (4oz), cut into thin strips, optional
Pitted black olives 16–20, chopped

1 Put the rice into a saucepan, add 400ml (14fl oz) cold water and bring to the boil. Reduce the heat to very low, cover the pan with a tight-fitting lid and cook gently for 25–30 minutes, or until the rice is cooked and has absorbed all of the water.

2 Meanwhile, preheat the grill to hot. Cook the peppers under the grill, turning them frequently until just softened and the skin is lightly browned and blistered. Put into a bowl, cover and, when cool, peel and deseed and cut into thin strips lengthways. Roughly chop the prawns and put into a bowl, then mix in the lemon zest and juice and add the Tabasco sauce to taste.

3 When the rice is cooked, gently mix in the rice vinegar and Wasabi paste, and then allow it to cool, but not completely. Then place a bamboo rolling mat on the worksurface with the slats parallel to you. Place one sheet of nori on the rolling mat, 2.5cm (1in) in from the edge nearest to you. Then, 2.5cm (1in) from the edge of the nori, spread over one-fifth of the rice, parallel with the edge and 6cm (2½in) wide.

4 Then arrange one-fifth of each of the remaining ingredients in adjacent rows along the centre of the rice. With the aid of the mat and starting at the edge nearest to you, very carefully roll up the nori, enclosing the filling as you go. When finished, very gently roll the mat backwards and forwards to make a neat roll. Leave in the mat while you make the next roll. Then, unwrap the first roll, wrap it in cling film, put on a tray and chill in the refrigerator. Repeat with the remaining nori sheets and filling.

5 When ready to serve, cut each roll into 8 slices using a very sharp, wet knife. Arrange on a dish and serve or cover and keep refrigerated until required. Serve as canapés or for supper with ice-cold Saki or a well-chilled dry white wine.

Preparation time **5 minutes**
Cooking time **10 minutes**
Calories per portion **184 Kcal**
Fat per portion **6g**
of which saturated **3.1g**
Serves **4**

Simple prawn sauté

There are many different types of prawns in the various seas of the world. Tiger prawns are harvested in the Indo-Pacific ocean, then transported to Britain. Prawns are a good source of iodine, needed for production of thyroxine in the thyroid gland to regulate the metabolism.

Cook's tip

Prawns can be thawed by placing the packaging in a bowl of cold water for a couple of hours.

Spray oil a few bursts
Spring onions 6, trimmed and chopped
Garlic 3 cloves, peeled and crushed
Dried mixed herbs a large pinch
Sherry 5 tbsp
Lemon juice 1 tbsp

Worcestershire sauce 2 tsp
Ready-to-eat tiger prawns 400g (14oz), thawed if frozen
Half fat crème fraîche 125ml (4fl oz)
Paprika for dusting

1 Spray a large frying pan with oil and add the spring onions and garlic. Season to taste and add the dried herbs. Fry for 3 minutes.

2 Pour the sherry, lemon juice and Worcestershire sauce into the pan. Stir well and then add the prawns. Cook for 2 minutes.

3 Add the crème fraîche. Lower the heat and cook gently for another 2 minutes. Serve on a bed of brown basmati rice, dusted with paprika.

Preparation time **20 minutes plus
10 minutes marinating**
Cooking time **20–25 minutes**
Calories per filo triangle **51 Kcal**
Fat per filo triangle **2g**
of which saturated **0.3g**
Makes **30 filo triangles**

Prawns in filo

This is a tasty and satisfying dish, which is excellent with a large mixed leaf and seed salad. The prawns are a fine source of lean protein and they also contain zinc, essential for over two hundred enzyme processes in the body.

Cook's tip

Filo pastry can dry out very quickly, making it difficult to use. To help prevent this from happening, keep a damp, clean cloth over the filo sheets that are waiting to be used.

Large, raw, peeled prawns 30 (approximately 350g (12oz)), thawed and drained well if frozen
Satay peanut sauce 50g (2oz)
Tomato ketchup 2 tbsp

Coriander 3 tbsp, chopped, plus extra to garnish
Reduced salt soy sauce 1 tbsp
Filo pastry 15 sheets
Olive oil 4 tsp

1 Rinse the prawns under a cold, running tap and then drain and dry them well on kitchen paper. In a large mixing bowl, blend together the peanut sauce, tomato ketchup, coriander and soy sauce. Add the prawns to the sauce and mix together gently. Cover the bowl and leave the prawns to marinate for 5–10 minutes.

2 Preheat the oven to 180°C/350°F/Gas 4. Lay the sheets of filo pastry in a pile on the worksurface with the short sides at the top and bottom. Cutting lengthways down the centre, divide the pile in two.

3 Take one strip of filo, lay it elsewhere on the worksurface and brush sparingly with olive oil. Place a prawn at the bottom end and to the left-hand side of the strip, nearest to you. Lift the right-hand corner of the pastry up and over the prawn to form a triangle. Then, fold the triangle directly up and over the next part of the filo.

4 Lift the left-hand corner and fold it over to the right – forming another triangle. Fold the triangle directly up again. Repeat the folding until the prawn is completely encased in the pastry strip. Place the wrapped prawn on a baking tray. Repeat Steps 3 and 4 with the remaining prawns and filo pastry strips.

5 Brush all the filled triangles with the remaining oil and bake for 15–20 minutes until the pastry is golden brown and crisp. Serve hot or cold garnished with some coriander leaves.

Preparation time **15 minutes**
Calories per portion **166 Kcal**
Fat per portion **3g**
of which saturated **0.4g**
Serves **4**

Florida prawn salad

The grapefruit was first introduced to Florida in 1823 by a French count and is still cultivated there today. This refreshing and pretty pink salad would make a lovely light meal at lunchtime or in the evening on a balmy summer's day.

Cook's tip

To save time, you can buy ready segmented grapefruit in natural juice in cans. Grapefruit also goes well with white fish and smoked fish, such as mackerel.

Pink grapefruit 2
Ready-to-eat tiger prawns 350g
(12oz), thawed if frozen
Endive, Swiss chard and radicchio salad mix 200g bag

Grapefruit marmalade 3 tbsp
Olive oil 2 tsp
White wine vinegar 2 tsp

1 Slice off the tops and bottoms of the grapefruits. Using a sharp knife, cut off the skin in downward slices taking away as much of the white pith as possible. Holding the fruit over a small bowl, slice in between the segments to remove the flesh and allow to fall in the bowl along with any juice.

2 Wash and pat dry the prawns and place in a bowl. Drain the grapefruit segments, reserving the juice, and toss into the prawns. Cover and chill until required.

3 When ready to serve, divide the salad mix between four serving plates and top with the prawns and grapefruit. Blend the marmalade with the reserved juice, oil and vinegar and add seasoning to taste. Spoon over the salad and serve immediately.

Preparation time **10 minutes plus
45 minutes proving**
Cooking time **30 minutes**
Calories per portion **181 Kcal**
Fat per portion **5g**
of which saturated **1.2g**
Serves **6**

Seafood pizza

Much more satisfying than a frozen pizza, this seafood version is delicious and nutritious. It has a cheese-free, pile-it-high topping that packs a punch with flavour. If you are short on time, you can make it using a ready-made base.

Cook's tip

Cooked pepper is available in cans and you can use 100g (3½oz) for this recipe. If you want to cook your own, see Mediterranean Pitta with Houmous on page 41.

Wholemeal bread mix 250g (9oz)
Chopped tomatoes 227g can
Large cooked red pepper 1
Tomato purée 2 tsp
Assorted cooked seafood 350g (12oz), thawed if frozen

Capers 1 tbsp, rinsed and chopped if large
Pitted black olives in brine 50g (2oz), drained
Olive oil 1 tsp
Lemon juice 1 tsp
Small basil leaves 1 tbsp

1 Preheat the oven to 220°C/425°F/Gas 7. Place the bread mix in a bowl and make up according to the packet's instructions.

2 Press the dough into a 25cm (10in) round and place on a baking sheet lined with baking parchment. Cover lightly and set aside to prove in a warm place for about 45 minutes or until doubled in size.

3 Meanwhile, place the tomatoes in a food processor. Roughly chop the pepper, discarding any seeds (and skin if preferred), and add to the tomatoes along with the tomato purée and seasoning to taste. Blend for a few seconds until smooth. Cover and chill until required.

4 Wash and pat dry the seafood. Spread the tomato mixture over the dough circle to within 1cm (½in) of the edge and pile the seafood evenly on top. Sprinkle the capers and olives over the top. Whisk together the oil and lemon juice and brush over the seafood. Bake in the oven for about 30 minutes until lightly golden and cooked through. Serve hot sprinkled with basil leaves.

Meaty
MAIN COURSES

Preparation time **5 minutes**
Cooking time **20 minutes**
Calories per portion **163 Kcal**
Fat per portion **5g**
of which saturated **2.5g**
Serves **4**

Easy chicken in mustard sauce

Chicken is a truly excellent source of protein, as it is low in fat and also contains useful vitamins and minerals. If you can afford to, choose organic free-range chicken, which has a much better flavour.

Cook's tip

Try this dish with thinly sliced sirloin steak in place of the chicken.

Spray oil a few bursts
Shallots 6 large, peeled and sliced
Chicken breasts 4 x 110g (4oz), cut into strips
Wholegrain mustard 1 tbsp
Half fat crème fraîche 6 tbsp

1 Spray a large pan with oil and gently fry the shallots, until they are transparent. Add the chicken and stir-fry for 6–8 minutes, until the chicken is cooked and browned all over.

2 Remove from the heat and add the mustard and crème fraîche. Reheat slowly for around 3 minutes, until piping hot. Serve with basmati rice or couscous and vegetables.

Preparation time **10 minutes plus 30 minutes marinating**
Cooking time **20 minutes**
Calories per portion **276 Kcal**
Fat per portion **7g**
of which saturated **2.4g**
Serves **4**

Lemon chicken with crushed potato

With its slightly aniseed flavour, tarragon is a great herb to use with poultry. This chicken dish has been served with a mixture of crushed potatoes and spring onions, a lovely way to add flavour and extra vitamins and a good alternative to traditional mash.

Cook's tip

Test the chicken is cooked by piercing it with the point of a knife – the juices should run clear. Do not be tempted to overcook the fillets or they will start to dry out.

Chicken breasts 4 x 110g (4oz)
Lemon 1, grated zest and 2 tbsp juice
Olive oil 4 tsp
Chopped tarragon 1 tbsp, plus extra to garnish

New potatoes 500g (1lb 2oz), scrubbed
Semi-skimmed milk 4 tbsp
Spring onions 4, trimmed and chopped
Dry white wine 90ml (3fl oz)
Half fat crème fraîche 4 tbsp

1 Remove any sinews from the chicken breasts and then cut the breasts in half horizontally. In a large non-metallic dish mix together the lemon juice, 2 teaspoons of the oil and the tarragon. Add the chicken breasts, making sure they are coated in the marinade and leave for 20–30 minutes.

2 Cook the potatoes in boiling water for about 15 minutes until just tender. Drain them, put them back in the pan with the milk and warm through. Add the rest of the oil and some seasoning. Crush the potatoes slightly with a potato masher or a fork, then add the spring onions. Keep the potatoes warm in the oven.

3 Meanwhile, heat a large pan. Remove the breasts from the marinade and cook over a medium heat for about 5 minutes, pressing them down with a spatula so that they brown evenly. Turn them over and cook for another 4 minutes.

4 Remove the cooked chicken from the pan and keep warm on a plate in the oven. Pour the wine into the hot pan, reduce it by about half and then, over a low heat, whisk in the crème fraîche.

5 Serve the chicken on hot plates on a bed of crushed potato with green beans. Spoon the sauce over and sprinkle with the lemon zest and a few more chopped tarragon leaves.

Preparation time **10 minutes**
Cooking time **30 minutes**
Calories per portion **252 Kcal**
Fat per portion **5g**
of which saturated **1.6g**
Serves **4**

Chicken & herb roulades

Poaching chicken in a mixture of stock and skimmed milk results in a creamy sauce, without the fat of a traditional cream sauce. The milk and quark add valuable calcium and the chicken provides magnesium and potassium.

Chicken breasts 4 x 110g (4oz), skinned
Quark 250g (9oz)
Pitted black olives 25g (1oz), chopped
Chopped basil leaves 2 tbsp
Chopped parsley 2 tbsp

Garlic 1 clove, peeled and crushed
Parma ham 4 slices
Chicken stock 300ml (½ pint)
Semi-skimmed milk 150ml (¼ pint)
Cornflour 2 tbsp

1 Place each chicken breast between two sheets of cling film and use the end of a rolling pin to beat them out to about double their original size.

2 To make the filling, mix together the quark, olives, basil, parsley and garlic. Divide this mixture between the chicken breasts. Roll the chicken breasts up to encase the filling, and then wrap a slice of Parma ham around each to keep them rolled up.

3 Pour the stock and milk into a deep frying pan or sauté pan. Add the roulades and place the pan over the heat. Bring to the boil, then cover the pan, reduce the heat and simmer the chicken for 10 minutes. Turn the roulades over and re-cover the pan and cook them for a further 10 minutes.

4 Remove the roulades from the pan. In a small container, mix the cornflour with 2 tablespoons of water. Bring the juices in the pan to the boil and stir in the slaked cornflour, mixing well to give a smooth sauce. Simmer the sauce for a couple of minutes to cook the cornflour.

5 Slice the chicken roulades and arrange on plates. Either pour over the sauce, or serve it separately in a jug. Serve the roulades with broccoli, runner beans and carrot sticks.

Cook's tip

The roulades may be made up to 6 hours in advance up to the end of Step 2. Keep them chilled until cooking.

Preparation time **15 minutes**
Cooking time **35 minutes**
Calories per portion **483 Kcal**
Fat per portion **7g**
of which saturated **2g**
Serves **4**

Southern-style chicken & chips

Treat yourself to a taste of the South with this easy meal. It may seem hard to believe that you can have chicken and chips when you're eating healthily, but with different preparation and a few adaptations, here's how you can ....

Cook's tip

Serve this diner-style supper with a crisp coleslaw salad tossed in a blend of light mayonnaise and low fat natural fromage frais.

Baking potatoes 2
Sweet potatoes 2
Spray oil a few bursts
Hot smoked paprika 1½ tsp
Dried onion granules 1½ tsp
Dried thyme 1½ tsp

Chicken quarters 4, skinned
Plain flour 2 tbsp
Egg 1, beaten
Dry white breadcrumbs 6 tbsp
Chopped thyme 1 tbsp
Tomato ketchup to serve

1 Preheat the oven to 220°C/425°F/Gas 7. Scrub the baking potatoes and peel the sweet potatoes. Cut into lengthwise chips about 1cm (½in) thick. Line two large baking sheets with baking parchment and arrange the chips evenly and well spaced out on top of one of them. Spray lightly with spray oil.

2 Mix together 1 teaspoon each of paprika, onion granules and dried thyme and sprinkle over the chips. Season to taste and bake for 30–35 minutes until tender, crisp and golden. Drain well.

3 Meanwhile, wash and pat dry the chicken. Mix the flour with the remaining paprika, onion granules and dried thyme, and season. Dust the chicken all over with the mixture.

4 On a plate, beat the egg with 2 tablespoons water, and place the breadcrumbs on another plate. Dip the chicken first in egg and then in crumbs to coat evenly. Place on the second prepared baking sheet. Spray with spray oil and bake for about 30 minutes until cooked through. Drain and keep warm.

5 To serve, pile the chips on warm serving plates and sprinkle with fresh thyme. Top with a piece of chicken and serve with Tomato Ketchup.

Preparation time **15 minutes plus marinating**
Cooking time **1 hour 20 minutes**
Calories per portion **292 Kcal**
Fat per portion **17g**
of which saturated **5.6g**
Serves **4**
Suitable for freezing

Soy spatchcock chicken

Roast chicken is one of Britain's favourite dishes. Here it has been marinated in citrus juice, honey and soy sauce to give a slightly oriental flavour. As much of the fat is contained in the skin, remove it before tucking in to this delicious Sunday roast.

Cook's tip

The preparation of the chicken is really quite easy – however, if preferred, a butcher will always do it for you.

Lemon 1 small, juice only
Lime 1, juice only
Clear honey 50g (2oz)
Reduced salt soy sauce 2 tbsp

Chicken 1.25 kg (2lb 8oz), rinsed under cold running water, and then dried with kitchen paper

1 To prepare the marinade, put the lemon and lime juice, honey and soy sauce into a large bowl and mix together well. To prepare the chicken, place the chicken breast-side down on a chopping board. Then – using poultry shears or a large, sharp, heavy knife – cut down each side of the backbone – If necessary, using a heavy kitchen weight to help cut through the bones. Remove and discard the bone.

2 Turn the chicken over and open it out flat, pressing lightly on the breastbone. Using a small, sharp, pointed knife, make a small cut through the skin at each side of the tip of the breastbone – approximately 2.5cm (1in) long. Insert the end of each leg through the holes made in the skin at the tip of the breastbone. Alternatively, keep the legs in place with a skewer. Put the chicken into the marinade and coat it well all over. Cover the bowl and refrigerate for 2–3 hours, or overnight if wished.

3 When ready to cook the chicken, heat the oven to 220°C/425°F/Gas 7. Remove the chicken from the refrigerator and place it, opened out, in a roasting tin. Pour any remaining marinade over the chicken and some water in the roasting tin so the honey juices don't burn. Cook in the centre of the oven for 30 minutes.

4 Reduce the heat to 180°C/350°F/ Gas 4 and cook for another 30 minutes, or until the chicken is cooked through, basting it frequently. Serve the chicken hot, accompanied with red cabbage cooked with apple or with new potatoes and a tossed green salad.

Preparation time **5 minutes**
Cooking time **25 minutes**
Calories per parcel **226 Kcal**
Fat per parcel **10g**
of which saturated **3.7g**
Makes **4 parcels**

Pork parcels

The inspiration for this recipe comes from the classic beef Wellington recipe, but pork has been substituted for the beef and it also uses filo pastry rather than 'naughty' puff pastry. These little parcels look very impressive and make a great dish for entertaining.

Spray oil a few bursts
Pork tenderloin 4 x 110g (4oz) pieces
Filo pastry 4 sheets, each 30x19cm (12x7½in)

Bottled red pimiento peppers 1 jar or 150g (5oz), well drained
Low fat garlic and herb soft cheese 50g (2oz)

1 Preheat the oven to 200°C/400°F/Gas 6. Spray a non-stick frying pan with two bursts of oil, add the pork and fry over a high heat for 5 minutes, turning until evenly browned on all sides. Leave to cool.

2 Cut one sheet of filo in half, spray one half with oil and then place the other half at an angle over the first. Put one piece of pimiento in the centre of the pastry and then put a piece of pork on top. Top with a quarter of the soft cheese and add another piece of pimiento.

3 Gather the pastry up and over the pork stack and pinch together to seal. Transfer to a baking sheet and repeat to make three more parcels.

4 Spray each pork parcel with a little extra oil and then bake for 20–25 minutes until the pastry is golden and the pork is thoroughly cooked through. Serve with roasted cherry tomatoes and green beans.

Cook's tip

Keep the filo pastry covered with a clean tea towel or plastic bag all the time that it's not being used as it does dry out very quickly, and once dry it will just crack when you try to use it.

Preparation time **5 minutes**
Cooking time **25 minutes**
Calories per portion **238 Kcal**
Fat per portion **7g**
of which saturated **2.3g**
Serves **4**

Sausage & red cabbage supper

Not only is it a very colourful vegetable, red cabbage is also a great source of vitamin C and of antioxidants, which have been shown to protect the brain against cell damage. The sausage and cabbage provide you with a substantial, yet simple meal.

Extra lean pork sausages 8
Spray oil a few bursts
Red onion 1, peeled and sliced
Red cabbage 275g (10oz), shredded

Juniper berries 10, crushed
Brown sugar 2 tbsp
Cider vinegar 1 tbsp
Apple juice 125ml (4fl oz)

1 Heat the grill to a medium-hot setting and cook the sausages until they are browned all over – about 10 minutes.

2 Meanwhile, spray a large pan with oil and gently fry the onion and cabbage together for 5 minutes.

3 Add the juniper berries and cook for a further 2 minutes. Add the sugar, vinegar, apple juice and sausages. Cook for 6–8 minutes, stirring occasionally. Serve with half a baked potato.

Cook's tip

Red onion has a sweeter, milder flavour than an ordinary onion. However, if red onion isn't available, the white variety will do just as well. The juniper berries, brown sugar and apple juice add a sweetness all of their own.

Preparation time **10 minutes**
Cooking time **1 hour 5 minutes**
Calories per portion **384 Kcal**
Fat per portion **26g**
of which saturated **12.1g**
Serves **4**

Lamb rack with spring vegetables

Rack of lamb is a bit pricey but it is very succulent. It makes a great roast when combined with a selection of spring vegetables. This dish would also work well with venison steaks or fillet, which are lower in fat and cholesterol.

Cook's tip

For a greater quantity of sauce, add some stock or vegetable water. If you find the stock is too thin then thicken with a little cornflour.

Young carrots 400g (14oz), trimmed and scrubbed
Shallots 8, peeled, optional
Garlic 4 cloves, optional
Thyme 2 sprigs
Rosemary 2 small sprigs
Olive oil 2 tsp

Juniper berries 12, coarsely crushed
Extra-lean racks of lamb 2 with a total weight of 550g (1lb 4oz)
Asparagus spears 12, woody ends trimmed
Redcurrant jelly 4 tsp
Red wine 150ml (¼ pint)

1 Preheat the oven to 200°C/400°F/Gas 6. Put the vegetables and herbs in a roasting tin, sprinkle with olive oil and mix them with your hands, to coat in oil. Roast for 25 minutes.

2 Meanwhile, press seasoning and the crushed juniper berries into the fleshy side of each lamb rack. Stir the roasting vegetables and add the asparagus.

3 Place the lamb racks flat and fat side up on top of the vegetables and cook for 20 minutes. Then spread 1 teaspoon of the redcurrant jelly over the lamb and cook for another 6 minutes. Remove the meat from the oven, wrap loosely in foil, set aside and leave to rest while you prepare the sauce.

4 Put the roast vegetables in a hot dish. Add the wine to the hot roasting tin, scraping up the cooking juices. Bring to the boil and whisk in the rest of the redcurrant jelly until thickened a little to make a small amount of glossy sauce.

5 Arrange the lamb on a serving plate, standing the racks on their thickest edge with the bones interlocking and the vegetables spooned around. Serve with the sauce in a warmed jug and new potatoes and cabbage.

Preparation time **15 minutes plus
30 minutes chilling**
Cooking time **15 minutes**
Calories per burger **340 Kcal**
Fat per burger **9g**
of which saturated **3.8g**
Makes **4 burgers**

Lamb burgers with apple relish

Perfect for a tasty supper or barbecue feast, these burgers are juicy and tender, and will be popular with everyone. The relish provides a refreshing mix of mint, apple and fromage frais, which complements the flavour of the meat.

Cook's tip

Vary the flavour of burger by replacing the lamb with minced turkey and use cranberry sauce instead of the mint flavours, or for a pork burger, why not use mango chutney instead?

Onion 1, peeled and finely chopped
Lean minced lamb 350g (12oz)
Dry wholemeal breadcrumbs 4 tbsp
Mint jelly 3 tbsp
Low fat natural fromage frais 4 tbsp
Chunky apple sauce 4 tbsp

Chopped mint leaves 1 tbsp
Wholemeal baps 4
Baby salad leaves a handful
Cucumber a few slices
Red onion a few slices, optional

1 Put the onion in a bowl. Add the lamb mince, breadcrumbs and 2 tablespoons of mint jelly. Season to taste and mix together thoroughly. Divide into four equal portions and form into 10cm (4in) burgers. Place on a plate lined with baking parchment and chill for 30 minutes.

2 For the relish, mix together the fromage frais, apple sauce, remaining mint jelly and chopped mint. Season lightly, cover and chill until required.

3 Preheat the grill to medium. Place the burgers on the grill rack and cook for 7–8 minutes on each side until cooked through. Drain and keep warm.

4 To serve, split the baps in half and top one half with a few salad leaves and some cucumber slices. Top with a burger, a spoonful of the apple relish and red onion slices, if using. Gently press the bap tops on the relish and serve immediately.

Preparation time **10 minutes**
Cooking time **20 minutes**
Calories per portion **404 Kcal**
Fat per portion **19g**
of which saturated **8.7g**
Serves **4**
Suitable for freezing

Minted Turkish meatballs

The combination of herbs and spices blended with minced meat and served with a yogurt sauce gives this dish a distinctly Turkish flavour. On a summer's evening, thread the meatballs onto skewers and cook on the barbecue.

Lean minced beef 450g (1lb)
Onion 1, peeled and finely chopped
Ground cumin ½ tsp
Ground coriander 1 tsp
Dried marjoram 1 tsp
Chopped parsley 2 tbsp

Egg 1, beaten
Butter 20g (¾oz)
Plain flour 4 tbsp
Semi-skimmed milk 300ml (½ pint)
Mint jelly 3–4 tbsp
Low fat natural yogurt 125g (4½oz)

1 Blend the beef, onion, spices and herbs in a food processor for a few seconds, until they are smooth.

2 Add the beaten egg and beat until smooth. With damp hands, divide the mixture into 20 portions and form into balls.

3 Dry fry or grill the meatballs for 7–10 minutes, turning frequently, until they are thoroughly cooked.

4 Meanwhile, place the butter, flour and milk in a saucepan and bring to the boil, whisking continuously. Season and then add the mint jelly and cook for 3 minutes. Cool the sauce by whisking, with the pan over a bowl of cold water. Add the yogurt and whisk well and then reheat very gently. Serve the sauce with the meatballs and little gem lettuce leaves, red onion slices, black olives and mint leaves.

Cook's tip

This recipe can also be cooked using turkey mince, which is leaner than beef. You can also try these meatballs threaded onto skewers with vegetables and grilled or barbecued.

Preparation time **15 minutes**
Cooking time **55 minutes**
Calories per portion **355 Kcal**
Fat per portion **10g**
of which saturated **2.9g**
Serves **2**

Steak & chips with watercress sauce

Bin the deep-fat-fryer and enjoy chips the healthy way. The steaks are complemented by the peppery flavour of watercress, which provides you with plenty of health promoting beta-carotene and calcium, required for stress management and healthy skin, nails and hair.

Cook's tip

You can actually cook the potatoes on a hot baking sheet on non-stick baking foil without any fat, although they do benefit from just a little oil to help them colour.

New potatoes 325g (11½oz), washed
Olive oil 2 tsp plus extra for brushing
Baby tomatoes on the vine 10
Watercress 100g pack or bunch

Sage leaves 2, optional
Low fat natural fromage frais 2–3 tbsp
Lean steak 2 x 150g (5oz), trimmed of any visible fat

1 Preheat the oven to 200°C/400°F/Gas 6. Put a heavy baking sheet in the oven to heat up. Cut the potatoes into quarters lengthways. Put them into a pan of boiling water and cook for 8–10 minutes until just tender.

2 Drain the potatoes well and dry a little in the pan over the heat. Add the oil to the pan, shake the potatoes, then spread them out on the hot baking sheet. Bake them for 40–45 minutes until browned, turning over halfway through cooking. Put the tomatoes on the baking sheet with the chips 5 minutes before the end of cooking.

3 Keep a good handful of the best watercress sprigs (put in a plastic bag) to serve with the steak. Strip the leaves off the stalks from the rest and chop them, along with the sage leaves, if using. Mix with the fromage frais.

4 Heat a griddle or heavy based frying pan and brush or spray it with a little oil. Flatten the steaks a little to make them even all over, if necessary. Season them and cook for a few minutes on each side, depending on how you like them.

5 Serve the steak and chips and roasted tomatoes garnished with the watercress and accompanied with the watercress sauce.

Preparation time **15 minutes plus
20 minutes marinating**
Cooking time **4–6 minutes**
Calories per portion **347 Kcal**
Fat per portion **15g**
of which saturated **4.9g**
Serves **4**

Meaty twizzle sticks with coleslaw

The crunchy, creamy coleslaw provides a wonderful contrast in texture to the succulent meat. Celeriac is a type of celery with a knobbly root that looks a bit like a turnip. It adds an unusual flavour and contains minerals such as potassium and phosphorus.

Cook's tip

To prevent the wooden skewers from burning, soak them in water for 10 minutes before using.

Sirloin steak 4 thin slices, trimmed of any visible fat
Pork tenderloin 250g (9oz), all visible fat removed
Thick-cut marmalade 3 tbsp
Wholegrain mustard 2 tbsp
Savoy cabbage ½, shredded

Carrots 3, peeled and grated
Celeriac ½, peeled and grated
Spring onions 2, trimmed and thinly sliced
Half fat crème fraîche 3 tbsp
Light mayonnaise 3 tbsp

1 Cut the sirloin steaks into eight strips. Cut the pork tenderloin into four long slices and then cut each slice in half lengthways. Put the marmalade and mustard into a large mixing bowl and blend. Add the beef and pork strips and mix gently with the marinade until well coated. Cover and leave for 15–20 minutes.

2 To make the coleslaw, put the remaining ingredients into a bowl. Mix well, cover the bowl and set aside until required.

3 To assemble the wooden skewers, take a strip of beef and a strip of pork and thread onto a skewer together, twisting them from side to side as you do so. Repeat with seven more wooden skewers.

4 Cook the skewered meat in a lightly oiled, large frying pan for 3–4 minutes, turning the skewers frequently until the meat is just cooked through. When the meat is nearly cooked, add the remaining marinade and turn the skewers until the meat is evenly coated.

5 Spoon the coleslaw into four bowls, arrange the twizzle sticks on top and serve immediately with crusty, seeded bread or new potatoes.

Preparation time **5 minutes**
Cooking time **10 minutes**
Calories per portion **200 Kcal**
Fat per portion **6g**
of which saturated **2.1g**
Serves **4**

Beef in black bean sauce

Made from fermented soya beans, black bean sauce is a traditional oriental flavouring, which works well with beef. The ginger and bamboo shoots are a good source of potassium, essential for regulating the body's cell function.

Sesame oil 1 tsp
Root ginger 1cm (½in) piece, peeled and grated
Garlic 2 cloves, peeled and crushed
Sirloin steak 400g (14oz), trimmed of any visible fat and thinly sliced
Red pepper 1, deseeded and sliced into long sticks

Courgette 1, trimmed and sliced into long sticks
Bamboo shoots 225g can, drained
Black bean sauce 3 tbsp
Hot beef stock 100ml (3½fl oz)
Bean sprouts 300g (11oz)

1 Heat the oil in a large frying pan or wok and add the ginger, garlic and steak. Stir-fry for around 3 minutes until the beef is browned all over.

2 Add the pepper, courgette, bamboo shoots, black bean sauce and beef stock and cook for a further 3 minutes.

3 Add the bean sprouts and stir-fry for another minute and then serve the beef mixture on a bed of noodles.

Cook's tip

Two 'nests' of noodles should be sufficient quantity to serve with this succulent dish.

Preparation time **15 minutes**
Cooking time **1 hour**
Calories per portion **320 Kcal**
Fat per portion **17g**
of which saturated **6.5g**
Serves **4**
Suitable for freezing

Spiced beef bake

This fruity, slightly spicy dish is a good source of protein and calcium. It is a hearty, warming dish that is ideal eaten after a brisk, refreshing walk in the British countryside enjoying the landscape and keeping fit at the same time!

Cook's tip

If you are trying to limit your fat intake, drain the meat in a sieve before adding the onion and chilli powder. This will help to remove some of the fat that escapes during cooking.

Lean minced beef 450g (1lb)
Onion 1, peeled and chopped
Garlic 1 clove, peeled and finely chopped
Curry paste or powder 4 tsp
Red or white wine vinegar 1 tbsp
Tomato purée 1 tbsp

Ready-to-eat dried apricots 40g (1½oz), chopped
Banana 1, peeled and chopped
Fresh breadcrumbs 50g (2oz)
Eggs 2
Semi-skimmed milk 125ml (4 fl oz)
Flaked almonds to garnish

1 Preheat the oven to 190°C/375°F/Gas 5 and lightly oil a round ovenproof dish that measures 13cm (5in) across and 9cm (3in) deep.

2 Heat a large, non-stick frying pan and dry-fry the minced beef and onion. Remove the pan from the heat and stir the garlic, curry paste or powder, vinegar, tomato purée, apricots, banana and breadcrumbs into the mince and season to taste. Spoon carefully into the prepared dish. Press down firmly and level the top. Cover with foil and bake for 40–45 minutes.

3 Whisk together the eggs and milk. Remove the dish from the oven, take off the foil and pour the eggs and milk over the meat. Scatter with flaked almonds and then return to the oven for 20–25 minutes (cover with foil if it is browning too quickly), until set. Serve with roasted carrots, swede and parsnips.

Great grains &
PERFECT PASTA

Preparation time **20 minutes plus soaking**
Cooking time **35 minutes**
Calories per portion **136 Kcal**
Fat per portion **3g**
of which saturated **0.2g**
Serves **4**
Suitable for vegetarians

Moroccan stuffed tomatoes

Moroccan food typically has a sweet and spicy taste, due to the addition of certain spices that were introduced to the country by the Arabs. This Moroccan-influenced dish contains spices along with couscous – the staple carbohydrate food from this region.

Cook's tip

You can use this couscous filling to stuff other vegetables, such as peppers, courgettes or aubergines.

Large beefsteak tomatoes 4
Couscous 100g (3½oz)
Red onion 1
Lemon juice 1 tbsp
Olive oil 1 tsp

Cooked chickpeas 110g (4oz)
Ground cinnamon 1 tsp
Ground cumin 1 tsp
Chopped coriander 3 tbsp

1 Preheat the oven to 190°C/375°F/Gas 5. Slice the tops off the tomatoes and scoop out and reserve the pulp and seeds. Stand the tomatoes upside down on kitchen paper to absorb some of the liquid. Set aside. Chop the tomato pulp, discarding the core, drain off the excess juice and set aside.

2 Soak the couscous according to the packet's instructions and set aside.

3 Meanwhile, peel and finely chop the onion and toss in the lemon juice. Heat the olive oil and gently cook the onion with the juice for 3–4 minutes until it has just softened.

4 Transfer the couscous to a mixing bowl and stir in the onion, the reserved tomato pulp, chickpeas, spices and coriander and season to taste.

5 Pack the couscous mixture into the tomato shells and replace the tomato tops. Stand in a small roasting tin and pour in just enough water to cover the bottom of the tin. Cover with foil and bake for 20 minutes. Remove the foil and bake for a further 10 minutes until tender. Drain and serve immediately.

Preparation time **15 minutes**
Cooking time **30–40 minutes**
Calories per portion **350 Kcal**
Fat per portion **4g**
of which saturated **1.4g**
Serves **4**
Suitable for freezing

Lemon chicken with couscous

The citrusy tang of lemon works wonderfully with chicken, which is a great source of low fat protein. The pieces of artichoke and courgette add delicate, yet delectable, flavours to this easy and nutritious dish.

Cook's tip

For an attractive stripy finish to the courgettes, use a peeler to remove strips of skin along the length of the vegetable before slicing.

Plain flour 25g (1oz)
Spray oil a few bursts
Ready jointed chicken pieces 1.4kg (3lb), skinned
Courgettes 250g (9oz), trimmed and thickly sliced

Artichoke hearts 390g can, drained and cut into halves or quarters
Lemon 1, grated zest and strained juice
Chicken stock 375ml (13fl oz)
Couscous 200g (7oz)
Coriander a few sprigs, for sprinkling

1 Put the flour on a large plate and add seasoning to taste. Very lightly coat the chicken pieces in the flour, shaking off the excess.

2 Heat the oil in a large, non-stick frying pan. Add the chicken pieces and cook them until lightly browned all over.

3 Add the courgettes, artichoke hearts, lemon zest and juice, and the chicken stock to the pan and bring to the boil, stirring continuously. Reduce the heat, cover and cook the chicken and vegetables gently for 15–20 minutes until the chicken is cooked through, but taking care not to over cook it.

4 Meanwhile, put the couscous into a saucepan, add 400ml (14fl oz) water and bring to the boil. Turn off the heat, cover the pan and leave to stand for 6–7 minutes, until the grains are swollen and all the water has been absorbed. Keep warm until the chicken is cooked.

5 Using a fork, fluff up the couscous to separate the grains. Serve the couscous, topped with the chicken, and scattered with coriander.

Preparation time **10 minutes**
Cooking time **1 hour 30 minutes**
Calories per portion **309 Kcal**
Fat per portion **8g**
of which saturated **3.5g**
Serves **4**
Suitable for freezing

Lamb & apricot couscous

A Moroccan inspired dish, this recipe is packed with flavour and really is an all-in-one meal, providing you with protein, carbohydrate, fibre, vitamins and minerals. It is quick to prepare and then you can forget about it while it cooks to perfection.

Spray oil 2–3 bursts
Lean lamb 350g (12oz), diced
Onion 1, peeled and sliced
Ground cinnamon 1 tsp
Ground turmeric 1 tsp
Leek 1, washed and sliced
Red pepper 2, deseeded and roughly chopped

Ready-to-eat dried apricots 150g (5oz)
Lemon 1, grated zest and juice
Lamb stock 450ml (¾ pint)
Couscous 110g (4oz)
Chopped flat leaf parsley 2 tbsp

1 Heat a saucepan or flameproof casserole dish and then spray with olive oil. Add the lamb and onion to the pan in a single layer. Cook over a high heat, turning occasionally until the lamb is browned on all sides. Add the cinnamon and turmeric and cook for a further minute, stirring well.

2 Add the leek, red pepper, apricots and lemon zest and juice to the casserole dish and mix with the meat. Pour the stock into the dish. Bring to the boil, then reduce the heat, cover the pan and leave to simmer gently for 1¼–1½ hours, or until the lamb is tender.

3 Add the couscous, stir and re-cover the pan. Continue to cook for a further 3–5 minutes, over a very gentle heat until the couscous is just tender and has thickened the juices. Stir the parsley into the mixture. Serve with a green salad.

Cook's tip

This recipe is versatile – it may also be cooked in a moderate oven rather than on the hob.

Preparation time **30 minutes plus
40 minutes cooling**
Cooking time **30 minutes**
Calories per portion **336 Kcal**
Fat per portion **6g**
of which saturated **1.7g**
Serves **4**
Suitable for vegetarians

Tomatoey polenta & ratatouille

If you have not tried polenta before, you really should give it a go. It is easy to cook and provides a low fat yet filling meal, which is perfect for non-meat eaters. The tomato, olive and basil flavours work wonderfully well and taste typically Italian.

Cook's tip

For a vegetarian meal, choose a cheese similar to Parmesan, which is suitable for vegetarians. Traditional Parmesan contains animal rennet.

Dry pack sun-dried tomatoes 50g (2oz), finely chopped
Salt 1 tsp
Dried oregano 1 tsp
Hot smoked paprika 1½ tsp
Tomato purée 1 tbsp
Polenta 225g (8oz)
Spray oil a few bursts
Onion 1, peeled and chopped
Courgettes 2, roughly chopped

Peppers 1 red and 1 orange, deseeded and diced
Button mushrooms 110g (4oz), wiped and quartered
Garlic 2 cloves, peeled and finely chopped
Chopped tomatoes 400g can
Vegetable stock 150ml (¼ pint)
Basil leaves small bunch, torn (optional)
Parmesan-like shavings 25g (1oz)

1 Put the sun-dried tomatoes in a pan with the salt, oregano, 1 teaspoon of the paprika and the tomato purée. Add 900ml (1½ pints) of water and bring to the boil. Gradually add the polenta and stir while simmering to ensure there are no lumps. Cook for 3–4 minutes until the mixture is thick enough to support the spoon standing up. Allow to cool for 10 minutes.

2 Meanwhile, line a shallow 23cm (9in) diameter cake tin with cling film so it overlaps the sides of the tin. Pile the polenta into the tin and spread out evenly. Allow to cool for 30 minutes.

3 For the ratatouille, spray a frying pan with oil, add the onion and sauté until softened. Add the courgettes, peppers, mushrooms, garlic and the remaining paprika and fry for 2 minutes. Add the tomatoes and stock and bring to the boil. Cover and simmer for 20 minutes.

4 Turn the polenta onto a chopping board and peel off the cling film. Cut into eight wedges. Tear the basil into pieces, if using, stir into the ratatouille, and arrange the polenta wedges on top. Lightly spray with oil then sprinkle with the parmesan. Brown the polenta under a hot grill and and transfer to warmed serving bowls.

Preparation time **5 minutes**
Cooking time **25 minutes**
Calories per portion **510 Kcal**
Fat per portion **13g**
of which saturated **1.1g**
Serves **2**
Suitable for vegetarians

Cherry tomato risotto

Tomatoes are an excellent source of vitamin C, beta-carotene, lycopene and folic acid. Lycopene is a potent antioxidant and crucial for maintaining prostate health. Here, tomatoes are combined with vegetables, rice and stock to create a satisfyingly filling meal.

Cook's tip

The risotto is also good with a few mushrooms added at the beginning and simmered along with the onion and celery.

Condensed tomato soup 295g can
Vegetable stock 600ml (1 pint)
Onion 1, peeled and chopped
Garlic 1 clove, peeled and crushed
Celery 1 stick, finely chopped
Chopped oregano 2 tbsp, or 1 tsp dried

Risotto or Camargue red rice 150g (5oz)
Red cherry tomatoes 250g (9oz), halved
Parmesan-like cheese shavings to garnish
Oregano to garnish

1 Pour the tomato soup into a saucepan and add the vegetable stock, onion, garlic, celery and oregano. Bring to the boil and simmer gently for about 5 minutes.

2 Tip the rice into the pan and bring to a gentle simmer. Cook the rice slowly for 17–20 minutes, stirring it occasionally, until the rice is almost tender. If you are using Camargue red rice, this takes slightly longer to cook (up to 25 minutes), in which case you might need to add some more stock towards the end of cooking.

3 Stir in the halved tomatoes and cook for 2–3 minutes, or until the tomatoes have heated through. Season to taste. Serve garnished with Parmesan shavings and oregano and accompanied with a green salad.

Preparation time **10 minutes**
Cooking time **40 minutes**
Calories per portion **332 Kcal**
Fat per portion **5g**
of which saturated **2.3g**
Serves **4**

Smoked haddock & pea risotto

Containing less butter than an Italian risotto, this dish is still very tasty with its smoky-flavoured fish, fresh herbs and tart capers. Unfortunately, peas lose their nutrients very quickly and so, unless you grow your own, frozen peas are more nutritious.

Cook's tip

Use fennel as well as – or instead of – the onion, as the flavour goes really well. If you don't want to use another pan, just stir the halved tomatoes into the risotto a few minutes before the end of cooking.

Onion 1, peeled and sliced
Garlic 1–2 cloves, peeled and crushed
Hot fish or vegetable stock 900ml (1½ pints)
Smoked haddock 350g (12oz)
Risotto rice 225g (8oz)
Frozen peas 110g (4oz)

Butter 15g (½oz)
Lemon ½, juice only
Capers 2 tbsp, rinsed and chopped if large
Chopped parsley 4 tbsp
Cherry tomatoes 12, halved
Lemon wedges to serve

1 Put the onion and garlic in a large, shallow saucepan with 300ml (½ pint) of the stock and put the fish, skin-side up, on top. Cover and simmer gently for 5 minutes until the fish is just cooked.

2 Remove the fish from the pan and set it aside. Then stir the rice into the pan and pour in half the remaining stock. Cook, uncovered, until the stock is almost absorbed, then add the rest of the stock.

3 Skin and check the fish for bones. Break it into large flakes. When the stock is almost absorbed again, stir in the peas, flaked fish, butter, lemon juice, capers and half the parsley. Add seasoning to taste.

4 Heat a small frying pan, add the cherry tomato halves and let them cook for 2–3 minutes until just softened.

5 When the rice is cooked and the fish is warmed through, top with the hot tomatoes and remaining parsley. Serve with lemon wedges.

Preparation time **15 minutes**
Cooking time **30–35 minutes**
Calories per portion **278 Kcal**
Fat per portion **6g**
of which saturated **0.5g**
Serves **4**
Suitable for vegetarians

Indian vegetable pilaff

This recipe uses Moglai curry paste, which has a medium strength flavour. Moglai curries were originally expensive creations cooked for the Moghul emperors. If you prefer, use a different paste, or even sun-dried tomato paste for a Mediterranean flavour.

Cook's tip

If you can't find Moglai curry paste, use the same quantity of jalfrezi paste instead.

Corn oil 1 tbsp
Onion 1 large, peeled and finely chopped
Hot red chilli 1 small, deseeded and finely sliced
Root ginger 1cm (½in) piece, peeled and grated
Long grain rice 175g (6oz)

Moglai curry paste 2–3 tbsp
Vegetable stock 600ml (1 pint)
Aubergine 1, trimmed and cubed
Baby corn 175g (6oz)
Frozen peas 110g (4oz)
Okra 150g (5oz), sliced, optional
Coriander handful, to garnish

1 Heat the oil in a large, shallow (lidded) frying pan. Add the onion and cook gently for 6–8 minutes, until softened but not browned.

2 Stir the chilli and ginger into the onion and cook for 1–2 minutes. Then stir in the rice and curry paste, add the stock and bring to the boil.

3 Mix the aubergine into the rice, cover the pan with a tightly fitting lid, reduce the heat to low and cook for 20–25 minutes, until the rice is almost but not quite cooked, topping up with a little extra stock if needed.

4 Using a fork, gently mix the corn, peas and okra (if using) into the rice and then continue cooking for another 10 minutes, until the rice is cooked. Garnish with torn coriander leaves and serve immediately with a side salad made with thinly sliced onion rings and tomatoes, lightly sprinkled with seasoned rice vinegar.

Preparation time **10 minutes**
Cooking time **15 minutes**
Calories per portion **319 Kcal**
Fat per portion **10g**
of which saturated **2.6g**
Serves **4**
Suitable for vegetarians

Spring vegetable pasta

Light and colourful with seasonal vegetables – just add what is freshest – this dish is packed with fibre, iron and other blood-boosting and antioxidant nutrients. If you are not watching fat too closely, serve with a piece of wholemeal garlic bread.

Cook's tip

To toast pine nuts, heat a small frying pan, add the pine nuts and stir over a medium heat until evenly coloured. Don't walk away from them!

Pasta, e.g. penne, twists or bows 225g (8oz)
Asparagus spears 8, woody ends trimmed and the spears cut into 5cm (2in) lengths
Peas, fresh or frozen 110g (4oz)
Spinach 110g (4oz), washed and drained and torn into strips

Half fat crème fraîche 5 tbsp
Capers 1 tbsp, rinsed and chopped if large
Lemon juice 1 tsp
Mint leaves a handful, shredded
Basil leaves a handful, shredded
Toasted pine nuts 3 tbsp

1 Add the pasta to a large pan of boiling water. Stir well and when it comes back to the boil, cook for 5 minutes. Add the asparagus, bring back to the boil and add the peas, then simmer another 3–4 minutes until the pasta is just getting tender.

2 Drain the pasta well. Put the spinach in the pasta pan and tip the pasta and vegetables on top. Stir gently so that the spinach starts to wilt.

3 Stir in the crème fraîche, capers and lemon juice and add seasoning to taste, keeping the pan over a low heat for a couple of minutes to heat everything through. Add the shredded mint and most of the shredded basil leaves.

4 Spoon the pasta mixture into hot serving dishes and sprinkle with pine nuts and the rest of the basil leaves. Serve immediately while hot.

Preparation time **5 minutes**
Cooking time **15 minutes**
Calories per portion **272 Kcal**
Fat per portion **12g**
of which saturated **6.2g**
Serves **2**
Suitable for vegetarians

Macaroni cheese with tomatoes

This one-pan meal is very quick to make and is a colourful supper dish. It is also good with any pasta, not just macaroni. You can try it with pasta bows or spaghetti or, for extra fibre, use a wholewheat pasta.

Cook's tip

For a more colourful recipe, use half red and half yellow cherry tomatoes and instead of using yogurt, substitute a small carton of low fat natural fromage frais in its place.

Macaroni 175g (6oz)
Cherry tomatoes 200g (7oz), halved
Spring onions 4, trimmed and sliced
Low fat natural yogurt 150g (5oz)

Mature Cheddar cheese 50g (2oz), grated
Basil a small handful of leaves, shredded, plus 2 sprigs to garnish

1 Cook the pasta in boiling water for 10–12 minutes, or according to the packet's instructions, until it's just tender. Drain the pasta into a sieve or colander.

2 Add the tomatoes and spring onions to the hot saucepan and cook them over a medium heat for 1–2 minutes to warm them through. Add the yogurt and half the Cheddar cheese to the pan and warm until the cheese just melts, but take care not to overheat the sauce, or it will separate.

3 Preheat the grill to hot. Return the pasta to the pan, and add the shredded basil and seasoning to taste and stir well. Transfer into a shallow ovenproof dish, sprinkle the rest of the cheese over the top and then grill for 3–5 minutes until the topping is golden. Serve immediately, garnished with basil leaves and accompanied with a green salad.

Preparation time **10 minutes**
Cooking time **15 minutes**
Calories per portion **326 Kcal**
Fat per portion **8g**
of which saturated **0.9g**
Serves **2**

Fish & noodle bowl

It might look like a long list of ingredients, but this is a quick and nourishing dish. It has a refreshing, light Thai flavour and is bursting with nutrients. Spring greens are an excellent source of vitamin C, beta-carotene and a variety of minerals, including calcium and iron.

Cook's tip

Use a pack of stir-fry vegetables for speed if you like or add any other vegetables, such as red pepper strips, sweetcorn and bean sprouts, if you can buy them very fresh.

Fish or chicken stock 600ml (1 pint)
Root ginger 1cm (½in) piece, peeled and grated
Red chilli 1, deseeded and finely sliced
Garlic 1 clove, peeled and finely chopped
Green or runner beans 150g (5oz), cut into short lengths
Monkfish 225g (8oz), cut into bite-sized cubes
Straight-to-wok traditional medium noodles 150g pack

Pak choi or spring greens 150g (5oz), finely shredded
Spring onions 4, trimmed and thinly sliced
Thai or fish sauce 1 tbsp
Lime ½, squeezed and drained juice
Pinch of sugar
Coriander leaves handful
Unsalted toasted cashew nuts 25g (1oz), chopped, to serve
Lime wedges to serve, optional

1 Heat the stock in a large pan with the ginger, chilli and garlic. When it comes to the boil, add the beans and cook for 2 minutes.

2 Add the monkfish then, when the stock comes back to the boil, stir in the noodles and put the pak choi or spring greens and spring onions on top. Leave to simmer for 3 minutes until the pak choi has just wilted. Then add the fish sauce, lime juice and sugar.

3 Use a draining spoon to serve the fish, noodles and vegetables into four hot, deep serving bowls. Pour or ladle the broth on top and sprinkle with coriander leaves, either whole or chopped, and cashew nuts. Place a lime wedge on the side, if you like. Eat the fish, vegetables and noodles with a fork and then use a spoon to eat the broth.

Preparation time **20 minutes**
Cooking time **45 minutes**
Calories per portion **435 Kcal**
Fat per portion **9g**
of which saturated **2.2g**
Serves **4**

Seafood in pasta shells

These huge pieces of pasta are perfect for stuffing with lots of yummy ingredients. Here we have used shellfish, which is a good source of zinc, the mineral that is crucial for the immune system and helps us process the food we eat.

Olive oil 1 tbsp, plus extra
Conchiglioni (large pasta shells) 24
Onion 1 large, peeled and chopped
Garlic 1 clove, peeled and crushed
Chopped tomatoes 400g can
Chopped oregano 1–2 tbsp
Frozen cooked mussels 150g (5oz), thawed and drained

Frozen large peeled prawns 225g (8oz), thawed, drained and chopped
Scallops 150g (5oz), thawed, drained and diced
Parmesan cheese 25g (1oz), grated
Fresh white breadcrumbs 15g (½oz)
Basil leaves for sprinkling

1 Bring a large saucepan of water to the boil and add 1 teaspoon of the olive oil. Add the pasta, stir gently, and then reduce the heat to low and simmer gently for 20–25 minutes until cooked.

2 Meanwhile, heat the remaining oil in a large saucepan and add the onion and garlic. Cook gently until the onion has softened, but not browned. Add the tomatoes and oregano and bring to the boil, then reduce the heat and cook gently, partially covered, for 20–25 minutes. Remove from the heat and let the sauce cool a little.

3 Place a colander in the sink and pour the pasta shells into it (taking care not to break them), and rinse under a slow, cold running tap to cool them down. Drain well.

4 Meanwhile, preheat the oven to 220°C/425°F/Gas 7. Very lightly oil a large shallow baking dish or four individual gratin dishes.

5 Mix the mussels, prawns and scallops into the tomato sauce. Then, carefully spoon the mixture into the pasta shells and place in the oiled dish or dishes.

6 Mix the cheese and breadcrumbs, sprinkle over the shells and bake for 15–20 minutes until piping hot and the topping is melted and browned. Sprinkle with basil and serve immediately, accompanied by a crisp, green salad.

Cook's tip

The pasta shells may be filled ahead of time and kept, covered, in the refrigerator ready for sprinkling with the cheese mixture and baking when they are required.

Preparation time **35 minutes**
Cooking time **35 minutes**
Calories per portion **404 Kcal**
Fat per portion **13g**
of which saturated **7.6g**
Serves **4**
Suitable for freezing

Tuna & sweetcorn lasagne

Tuna is an oily fish, which means that it's high in essential fatty acids, which are vital for keeping our skin healthy and for helping to combat osteoarthritis. The tuna and sweetcorn have been used in place of minced beef for a healthier version of traditional lasagne.

Cook's tip

For a vegetarian version of this dish, simply steam a mixture of vegetables of your choice and use them in place of the tuna.

Chopped tomatoes with herbs 400g can
Onion 1, peeled and chopped
Mushrooms 50g (2oz), wiped and sliced
Garlic 1 clove, peeled and crushed
Fresh lasagne 5 sheets
Tuna in spring water 400g can, drained and flaked

Canned sweetcorn 110g (4oz), drained
Semi-skimmed milk 450ml (¾ pint)
Flour 40g (1½oz)
Butter or margarine 25g (1oz)
Mature Cheddar cheese 50g (2oz), grated

1 Preheat the oven to 200°C/400°F/Gas 6. Place the tomatoes, onion, mushrooms and garlic into a large saucepan and bring to the boil. Simmer for 3 minutes.

2 Meanwhile, place the lasagne sheets into a pan of boiling water. Bring back to the boil and then turn off the heat and leave for 2 minutes. Drain well.

3 Stir the tuna and sweetcorn into the tomato mixture and pour half of it into the bottom of a lasagne dish. Place 3 of the lasagne sheets on top. Pour the rest of the tuna mixture into the dish and top with the remaining lasagne.

4 Place the milk, flour and butter or margarine in a saucepan and bring to the boil, whisking continuously. Turn down the heat and cook for a further minute. Take off the heat and add half of the cheese. Stir until the cheese melts.

5 Pour the cheese sauce onto the lasagne and then sprinkle with the remaining cheese. Bake for 35–40 minutes until golden and the cheese is bubbling. Serve with a large green salad.

Preparation time **10 minutes**
Cooking time **10 minutes**
Calories per portion **397 Kcal**
Fat per portion **8g**
of which saturated **1.1g**
Serves **2**

Tagliatelle savoy

The savoy cabbage is packed with vitamin C, folic acid, fibre and calcium, which help protect bones and may also help to prevent colon cancer. The anchovies add omega 3, and peas are rich in thiamin.

Cook's tip

For some extra flavour, add a clove or two of garlic with the anchovies and chillies. If you have any leftover anchovies, use them in the salsa to accompany the tuna steaks on page 87.

Tagliatelle 150g (5oz)
Frozen peas 50g (2oz)
Savoy or spring cabbage 150g (5oz), finely shredded
Anchovies 4 fillets, roughly chopped
Olive oil (or oil from can of anchovies) 1 tbsp

Red chilli 1, deseeded and finely chopped
Day old granary or white bread 1 slice, made into crumbs

1 Add the tagliatelle to a large pan of boiling water and cook for 6 minutes. Then add the peas and shredded cabbage and cook for 2–3 minutes more until the pasta is just tender.

2 Meanwhile, put the anchovies, oil and chilli in a small frying pan and fry for a minute. Then add the breadcrumbs and stir over a medium heat for a few more minutes until crunchy and golden.

3 Drain the pasta and vegetables and put them back in the pan, toss in three-quarters of the crumb mixture and add seasoning to taste. Serve the pasta in individual bowls and sprinkle with the rest of the crumbs.

Chicken & fennel pasta bake

Preparation time **15 minutes**
Cooking time **40 minutes**
Calories per portion **577 Kcal**
Fat per portion **23g**
of which saturated **12.2g**
Serves **4**

A sophisticated pasta dish that would be impressive to serve at a dinner party. Fennel has a delicate, sweet aniseed flavour, and it is a good source of vitamin C and potassium. Of course, you obtain plenty of calcium from this dish too.

Red onions 2, peeled and finely sliced
Lemon ½, ½ tsp grated zest and 1 tbsp juice
Fennel bulbs 2, trimmed and sliced into thin strips
Olive oil 2 tsp
Pasta, e.g. penne 225g (8oz)
Cooked boneless breast fillets of chicken 225g (8oz), chopped

Sultanas 50g (2oz)
Light soft cream cheese with garlic and chives 400g (14oz)
Semi-skimmed milk 4 tbsp
Chopped chives 2 tbsp
Low fat Mozzarella 75g (3oz), drained and thinly sliced

1 Preheat the oven to 200°C/400°F/Gas 6. Toss the red onions in the lemon juice.

2 Heat the oil in a large frying pan and gently fry the fennel and onion for 4–5 minutes, stirring, until beginning to soften. Transfer to a heatproof bowl, season to taste and set aside.

3 Bring a large saucepan of water to the boil and cook the pasta according to the packet's instructions until just cooked. Drain well and toss into the vegetables.

4 Add the chicken to the pasta along with the sultanas. Mix together the cheese and milk and stir into the pasta along with the chives and lemon zest.

5 Mix well and then pile into an ovenproof baking dish and place on a baking sheet. Arrange the mozzarella on top and bake in the oven for 20–25 minutes until golden.

Cook's tip

Accompany this filling dish with a simple sliced plum tomato, onion, wild rocket and fresh basil salad.

Preparation time **10 minutes**
Cooking time **50 minutes**
Calories per portion **145 Kcal**
Fat per portion **4g**
of which saturated **1.3g**
Serves **8**
Sauce suitable for freezing

Spaghetti with pork Bolognese sauce

Adding lots of vegetables makes a Bolognese sauce 'stretch' farther as well as being less fat per portion. There is no need to cook extra vegetables or serve a salad with this all-in-one meal, so it is really easy to prepare.

Cook's tip

Make a large batch of sauce then freeze it in portion sizes for quick suppers.

Lean minced pork 500g (1lb 2oz)
Onion 1, peeled and finely chopped
Carrot 1, peeled and finely diced
Red pepper 1, deseeded and diced
Garlic 1–2 cloves, peeled and finely chopped
Mushrooms 110g (4oz), wiped and chopped
Dried oregano or mixed herbs 1 rounded tsp
Bay leaves 2

Chopped tomatoes 400g can
Vegetable or chicken stock 225ml (8fl oz)
Tomato ketchup 1 tbsp
Green beans 110g (4oz), chopped into small pieces
Spaghetti 50g (2oz) per person
Chicken gravy granules 2 tsp
Grated Parmesan cheese to serve, optional

1 Heat a deep frying pan. Add the pork mince in one layer and cook over a medium heat for 5 minutes, turning it once so it browns all over.

2 Add the onion, carrot, red pepper and garlic and cook for 5 minutes, covered, before adding the mushrooms and herbs. Cook for another 5 minutes and then add the tomatoes and stock and stir in the ketchup and beans. Simmer, uncovered, for 20–30 minutes.

3 Bring a large saucepan of water to the boil and cook the spaghetti according to the packet's instructions.

4 A few minutes before serving, sprinkle the gravy granules into the mince to thicken the sauce and season to taste.

5 Drain the spaghetti, divide between hot bowls and spoon the sauce on top. Serve with grated Parmesan if you're not cutting down on fat too seriously.

Superb
STEWS

Preparation time **20 minutes**
Cooking time **45–50 minutes**
Calories per portion **134 Kcal**
Fat per portion **3g**
of which saturated **0.4g**
Serves **6**
Suitable for vegetarians + freezing

Chunky mixed vegetable stew

Choosing a variety of different coloured vegetables should also give you a good variety of vitamins and minerals. In this one-pot dish, there is a whole rainbow of colours to enjoy and to give your body plenty of nutrients.

Cook's tip

If you like, freeze the stew in single portions, which you can then gently reheat from frozen.

Olive oil 1 tbsp
Onions 250g (9oz), peeled and cut into 6 wedges
Garlic 1 clove, peeled and chopped
Potatoes 400g (14oz), peeled, washed and cut into 2.5cm (1in) cubes
Carrot 1 large, trimmed, peeled and thickly sliced
Courgettes 225g (8oz), trimmed and thickly sliced
Red pepper 1, deseeded and cut into thick slices

Green pepper 1, deseeded and cut into thick slices
Vegetable stock 300ml (½ pint)
Smoked paprika ½ tsp
Canned cherry or chopped tomatoes in natural juice 395g can
Savoy cabbage 150g (5oz), thickly shredded
Mangetout 75g (3oz), trimmed
Baby corn 75g (3oz)
Thin shavings of Wensleydale cheese to serve

1 Heat the olive oil in a very large saucepan, add the onions, garlic, potatoes and carrot and stir over a moderate heat for 2–3 minutes.

2 Add the courgettes and red and green peppers to the pan and stir for 1 minute. Pour the stock into the pan, add the smoked paprika and bring the stew up to the boil. Reduce the heat to low, cover the pan with a tight-fitting lid and cook for 15–20 minutes until the potatoes and carrots are almost but not quite cooked.

3 Gently mix the tomatoes, cabbage, mangetout and baby corn into the stew, then continue to cook gently for another 10–15 minutes until all the vegetables are cooked.

4 Add freshly ground black pepper to taste and serve sprinkled with Wensleydale cheese.

Preparation time **15 minutes**
Cooking time **15 minutes**
Calories per portion **301 Kcal**
Fat per portion **4g**
of which saturated **0.7g**
Serves **4**

Mediterranean-style fish stew

Half stew and half soup, this dish is a popular light meal in coastal regions of France, served simply with crusty French bread to mop up the sauce. Seafood is a good source of zinc, which helps make new cells and with the healing of wounds.

Cook's tip

Try toasting slices of French bread and rubbing with raw garlic. To eat, break pieces of the bread into the stew and push in gently to absorb the sauce.

Olive oil 1 tsp
Onion 1 large, peeled and chopped
Garlic 2 cloves, peeled and chopped
Bay leaf 1
Thyme, rosemary and oregano 1 sprig of each
Fish stock 350ml (12fl oz)
Dry white wine 150ml (¼ pint)

Firm white fish fillets, e.g. cod, halibut or monkfish 450g (1lb)
Fresh prepared mussels 450g (1lb)
Chopped tomatoes 400g can
Peeled prawns 225g (8oz), thawed if frozen
Chopped parsley 2 tbsp

1 Heat the oil in a large saucepan and gently fry the onion and garlic for 5 minutes, stirring, so they soften without browning. Set the onion and garlic to one side.

2 Tie together the bay leaf and herb sprigs and add to the saucepan. Pour the stock and wine into the pan.

3 Wash and pat dry the fish and cut the fillets into 2.5cm (1in) thick pieces and then add to the saucepan. Bring to the boil, add the mussels, cover and simmer for 5 minutes.

4 Carefully stir in the chopped tomatoes and prawns and add the cooked onion and garlic. Season to taste. Bring back to the boil, cover, reduce to a gentle simmer and cook for a further 3–4 minutes until piping hot, the fish is just cooked through and the mussels have opened.

5 To serve, discard the herbs and any mussels that haven't opened. Ladle into warmed serving bowls, sprinkle with parsley and serve immediately.

Preparation time **15 minutes**
Cooking time **2 hours**
Calories per portion **393 Kcal**
Fat per portion **23g**
of which saturated **6.7g**
Serves **6**

Pot-roast chicken in cider

This dish looks and tastes like old-fashioned country cooking, with all the flavours reliant on the quality of the ingredients, but without adding any fat. For the most flavour and best supply of nutrients, buy the best chicken you can afford.

Lemon ½, juice only
Whole free-range chicken 1.5 kg (3lb)
Onions 2, peeled and each cut into 8–12 wedges
Carrots 2, peeled and sliced
Garlic 2 cloves, peeled and sliced
Thyme sprigs 2 plus extra for garnish
Bay leaves 2

Cider 330ml bottle
Leeks 2, trimmed, washed and thickly sliced
Sugar snap peas 150g (5oz)
Butter 15g (½ oz) melted, optional
Cornflour or chicken gravy granules 1 tbsp

1 Squeeze the lemon juice over the chicken, rub it in well and then season to taste. In a large, heavy-based casserole, make a bed of the onions, carrots, garlic and herbs. Place the chicken, breast down, in the pot and pour the cider over the top. Cover and place over a medium heat. As soon as the juices begin to boil, after about 5 minutes, turn down the heat and leave to cook gently, without disturbing it, for 30 minutes.

2 Carefully turn the chicken over so the breast is up. Tuck the white part of the leeks around, cover again and cook for an hour until the juices run clear when the thigh of the chicken is pierced with a knife. Add the green part of the leeks and sugar snap peas for the last 10 minutes of cooking.

3 If you have an oven with an inbuilt grill, brown the chicken at the end of cooking by brushing the top with 15g (½oz) melted butter and grill for 3–4 minutes.

4 Lift out the chicken onto a serving plate, tipping any juices back into the casserole. Let the chicken rest in a warm place for 5–10 minutes. Spoon the vegetables out into a serving dish using a draining spoon. Bring the cooking juices to the boil, remove the herbs, and thicken with cornflour or gravy granules.

5 Cut the chicken into portions and arrange in hot individual dishes with a portion of the vegetables. Garnish with thyme and serve with the sauce.

Cook's tip

If you don't want to use cider, cook the chicken in the same quantity of apple juice or a mixture of the two, or use chicken stock.

Preparation time **10 minutes**
Cooking time **1 hour**
Calories per portion **444 Kcal**
Fat per portion **21g**
of which saturated **6.4g**
Serves **2**
Suitable for freezing

Winter warmer

As the title suggests, this easy meal is perfect to warm you up on a wintry evening or snowy weekend. At a time when locally produced vegetables are not found in abundance, the swede is readily available.

Cook's tip

If you do not like swede, substitute any other root vegetable, such as carrot, parsnip or celeriac, in its place.

Spray oil a few bursts
Chicken 4 thighs
Spring onions 1 bunch, trimmed and sliced

Lean smoked back bacon 4 rashers, trimmed of any visible fat and chopped
Swede ½, peeled and cubed
Vegetable stock 450ml (16fl oz)
Dijon mustard 1 tsp

1 Preheat the oven to 200°C/400°F/Gas 6. Spray a large frying pan with oil and fry the chicken thighs until browned all over. Remove with a slotted spoon and place in a casserole dish. Add the spring onions and bacon to the pan and sauté until the onion has softened and the bacon is cooked.

2 Spoon the onions and bacon into the casserole dish and add the swede, vegetable stock and mustard. Cover and cook for about an hour until the chicken and swede are thoroughly cooked.

3 Remove any skin from the chicken thighs and serve with a scoop of mashed potato.

Preparation time **15 minutes**
Cooking time **15 minutes**
Calories per portion **313 Kcal**
Fat per portion **6g**
of which saturated **1g**
Serves **4**
Suitable for freezing

Oriental chicken stew

This Chinese-style dish is low in fat but certainly not low in flavour. The ginger and soy sauce give a subtle kick to the taste of the other ingredients. For additional carbohydrate, serve on a bed of noodles.

Cook's tip

Jars of ready chopped ginger are available in the herb and condiments section of the supermarket. It is a lot easier to use than root ginger!

Olive oil 1 tbsp
Skinless chicken breasts 4 x 110g (4oz), cubed
Garlic 2 cloves, peeled and crushed
Root ginger 2.5cm (1in) piece, peeled and grated
Reduced salt soy sauce 1 tbsp
Vegetable stock 350ml (12fl oz)

Carrots 2 large, peeled and cut into strips
Mangetout 75g (3oz), trimmed and sliced lengthways
Spring onions 8, trimmed and sliced
Cornflour 2 tsp
Straight-to-wok noodles 300g (11oz)

1 Heat the oil in a large frying pan or wok and add the chicken, garlic, ginger and soy sauce. Fry gently over a low heat for 8–10 minutes, stirring, until the meat has browned all over.

2 Add the vegetable stock and carrots and cook for 3 minutes. Then add the mangetout and spring onions and cook for a further 3 minutes, until the vegetables are just tender.

3 To thicken the sauce, mix the cornflour to a smooth paste with a little water. Add to the stock and bring to the boil, stirring.

4 Meanwhile, cook the noodles following the packet's instructions. Strain the noodles and use to line four warmed bowls. Spoon the chicken and vegetables over the top and serve immediately while hot.

Preparation time **10 minutes**
Cooking time **35 minutes**
Calories per portion **445 Kcal**
Fat per portion **10g**
of which saturated **2.6g**
Serves **4**

Spicy pork, pasta & beans

An all-in-one pot recipe that's great for family cooking, but make sure it's a big pot! It provides fibre, protein and carbohydrate and so needs no accompaniment. If left to stand, the pasta will absorb the sauce, so if it gets too thick, just add boiling water and stir well.

Cook's tip

With the cumin seeds and chilli this dish could be quite spicy (depends on the chilli). Take the heat out by adding some tomato ketchup or sugar.

Olive oil 2 tsp
Pork fillet 375g (13oz), trimmed of any visible fat and sinew and cut into 1cm (½in) cubes
Onion 1, peeled and sliced
Green pepper 1, deseeded and sliced
Garlic 2 cloves, peeled and crushed
Red chilli 1, deseeded and finely chopped

Cumin seeds 2 tsp
Passata 500g (1lb 2oz)
Chicken stock 750ml (1¼ pints)
Pasta, e.g. penne 175g (6oz)
Cannellini beans 420g can, drained and rinsed
Chopped parsley 4 tbsp

1 Heat the oil in a deep saucepan, add the pork and let it colour all over for 5 minutes. Add the onion, green pepper, garlic and chilli and cook for another 5 minutes. Sprinkle cumin seeds into the pan and stir well. Cook for another minute.

2 Pour in the passata and stock, bring to the boil then add the pasta. Bring it back to the boil and add the beans and half the parsley. Season to taste and stir well.

3 Cook, uncovered, over a low to medium heat for 15 minutes, stirring occasionally, until the pasta is just tender and coated in a thick sauce (add a little hot water if the sauce gets too thick).

4 Sprinkle with the rest of the parsley and then let the stew stand for 5 minutes before serving straight from the pot.

Preparation time **15 minutes**
Cooking time **35 minutes**
Calories per portion **313 Kcal**
Fat per portion **14g**
of which saturated **4.6g**
Serves **4**
Suitable for freezing

Sausage, squash & root vegetables

Banish the winter blues with this chill-busting sausage dish. With lots of flavour, it's guaranteed to cheer you up, whatever the weather. Butternut squash is also known as winter squash and is a great antioxidant, which is thought to help fight against cancer.

Cook's tip

The stew is good enough to eat on its own, although you may want to serve it with freshly cooked green vegetables or some wholemeal pasta or brown rice.

Onion 1 large, peeled and chopped
Celery 2 sticks, trimmed and sliced
Parsnip 1, peeled and cut into small chunks
Carrot 1 large, peeled and cut into small chunks
Butternut squash ½ small

Beef stock 600ml (1 pint)
Low fat pork sausages 454g pack
Vegetable oil 1 tsp
Chopped tomatoes with garlic 400g can
Dried mixed herbs 1 tsp

1 Place the onion, celery, parsnip and carrot pieces in a large saucepan. Scoop out the seeds from the squash and cut in half. Slice off the skin and then cut into small chunks. Mix into the other vegetables and pour the stock over the top. Bring to the boil, cover and simmer for 10 minutes.

2 Meanwhile, slice each sausage into 3 equal pieces. Heat the oil in a frying pan until very hot and then stir-fry the sausage pieces for 3–4 minutes until golden all over. Remove from the pan and drain on kitchen paper.

3 Add the sausages to the vegetables and stir in the chopped tomatoes and herbs. Bring back to the boil and simmer uncovered for about 20 minutes, stirring occasionally, until tender, cooked through and thickened. Serve immediately while hot.

Preparation time **10 minutes**
Cooking time **1½ hours**
Calories per portion **366 Kcal**
Fat per portion **9g**
of which saturated **3.5g**
Serves **4**
Suitable for freezing

Lamb & barley stew

There is a generous amount of barley in this stew, which should provide sufficient starch, so you can serve it on its own without potatoes or rice. It's not necessary to pre-brown the meat, just put everything into a casserole dish, transfer to the oven and forget about it.

Cook's tip

This recipe may also be cooked on the hob. Bring the mixture to the boil, then reduce the heat, cover the pan and simmer it for about 1½ hours until the meat and vegetables are tender.

Lean lamb 350g (12oz), diced
Parsnips 2, peeled and chopped
Carrots 2, peeled and chopped
Swede 1 small, peeled and chopped
Onion 1, peeled and sliced

Red wine 150ml (¼ pint)
Lamb stock 450ml (¾ pint)
Pearl barley 110g (4oz)
Rosemary 2–3 sprigs

1 Preheat the oven to 160°C/325°F/Gas 3. Place all the ingredients, except the seasoning, into a casserole dish.

2 Cover the dish with a lid and place it in the oven for 1½–2 hours, or until the meat, barley and vegetables are tender. Season to taste and serve with steamed broccoli.

Preparation time **20 minutes**
Cooking time **2 hours**
Calories per portion **257 Kcal**
Fat per portion **9g**
of which saturated **3.5g**
Serves **4**
Suitable for freezing

Beef & tomato casserole

The combination of beef, carrots, tomatoes and garlic in this casserole ensures you are supplied with plenty of iron, vitamin A and potassium. Garlic is a potent antioxidant and also helps to reduce cholesterol, so be liberal with it in your cooking!

Spray oil a few bursts
Lean braising steak 500g (1lb 2oz), trimmed of any visible fat and cubed
Onions 2 large, peeled and chopped
Garlic 4 cloves, peeled and crushed
Lean bacon 4 rashers, trimmed of any visible fat and cut into strips

Baby carrots 150g (5oz), trimmed and scrubbed
Beef stock 300ml (½ pint)
Chopped tomatoes 400g can
Sage 4 leaves
Thyme 4 sprigs

1 Preheat the oven to 160°C/325°F/Gas 3. Spray a large non-stick pan with oil and add the braising steak. Brown the meat all over and then add the chopped onions, the garlic and the bacon. Reduce the heat, and cook for a further 5 minutes.

2 Spoon the meat and onions into a casserole dish and add the carrots. Pour the stock into the dish and add the chopped tomatoes. Add the herbs and then cover.

3 Cook in the oven for around 2 hours until the meat and vegetables are tender. Remove the herbs, season to taste and serve in warmed bowls with a chunk of wholemeal bread.

Cook's tip

Check the casserole every 30 minutes or so to ensure everything is cooking evenly – give the contents a good stir each time – and that the stew isn't drying out. You might need to add some extra stock to top it up.

Preparation time **15 minutes**
Cooking time **1½ hours**
Calories per portion **444 Kcal**
Fat per portion **13g**
of which saturated **4.3g**
Serves **6**
Suitable for freezing

Stout beef stew

This wholesome dish is pure comfort food! With minimal preparation, you can treat yourself to an hour or so with a good book while it cooks. Its flavours work wonderfully well with a scoop of mashed potato, mixed with a little wholegrain mustard.

Cook's tip

For a more hearty stew add some cubed potato along with the carrots.

Olive oil 2 tbsp
Onion 1 large, peeled and sliced
Plain flour 4 tbsp
Stewing steak 1.5kg (3lb), trimmed of any visible fat and cut into chunks

Bay leaves 2
Carrots 450g (1lb), peeled and chopped
Beef stock 600ml (1 pint)
Guinness 440ml can
English mustard 2 tsp

1 Preheat the oven to 180°C/350°F/Gas 4. Heat 1 tbsp of the olive oil in a large flameproof casserole dish. Add the onion and fry until softened.

2 Put the flour onto a plate and season to taste. Add the steak and coat with the flour. Add the floured steak chunks to the casserole and fry until browned all over.

3 Add the bay leaves, carrots, stock and Guinness and stir. Cover and place in the oven. Cook for 1 hour and then remove the lid and cook for a further 30 minutes. Season to taste and stir the mustard into the stew. Serve piping hot with mashed potatoes and peas.

Simple
SIDES

Preparation time **15 minutes**
Calories per portion **73 Kcal**
Fat per portion **1g**
of which saturated **0.1g**
Serves **4**
Suitable for vegetarians

Sunshine sprouting salad

A crunchy taste sensation that's good enough to eat on its own, or enjoy as an accompaniment to smoked fish or chicken. With the addition of fruit and yogurt, this salad is beneficial in many ways and also tastes great.

Cook's tip

Sprouting seeds are packed full of nutrition and are very tasty to eat. They are available chilled in bags from the greengrocer or health food shop.

Oranges 2
Carrot 1 large, peeled and grated
Radishes 110g (4oz), trimmed and thinly sliced
Wild rocket 50g (2oz)

Mixed bean sprouts 75g (3oz)
Alfalfa seed sprouts 50g (2oz)
Low fat natural yogurt 4 tbsp
Clear honey 2 tsp

1 Slice the tops and bottoms off the oranges. Using a sharp knife, cut off the skin in downward slices taking away as much of the white pith as possible. Holding the fruit over a small bowl, slice in between the segments to remove the flesh and allow to fall in the bowl along with any juice. Set aside.

2 In a mixing bowl, gently toss together the carrot, radishes, rocket and sprouts. Drain the orange segments, reserving the juice, and toss into the bowl. Cover and chill until required.

3 Mix the reserved juice with the yogurt, honey and add seasoning to taste. Cover and chill until required. To serve, pile the sprouting salad into individual serving dishes and drizzle with the yogurt dressing.

Preparation time **10 minutes**
Calories per portion **68 Kcal**
Fat per portion **2g**
of which saturated **0.3g**
Serves **2**
Suitable for vegetarians

Lime-dressed courgettes

This fresh salad has an oriental tang with the addition of the coriander, so it goes well with other eastern recipes, such as the Teriyaki griddled tuna on page 88. It is really quick to prepare and makes a much fresher alternative to boiled courgettes.

Cook's tip

Don't prepare this salad too far in advance or all the juices will come out of the courgettes and they will be very wrinkly.

Lime 1, grated zest and strained juice
Caster sugar 1 tbsp
Chopped coriander 2 tbsp
Olive oil 1 tsp
Boiling water 1 tbsp

Red chilli 1, deseeded and chopped, optional
Courgettes 2, trimmed and coarsely grated

1 To make the dressing, mix together the lime zest and juice, sugar, coriander, oil, water and chilli, if using.

2 Tip the courgettes into a bowl and then stir in the dressing. Leave the courgettes for a few minutes for the flavours to start to blend. Serve with the Teriyaki tuna recipe from page 88.

Preparation time **5 minutes**
Cooking time **10 minutes**
Calories per portion **60 Kcal**
Fat per portion **4g**
of which saturated **0.4g**
Serves **4**
Suitable for vegetarians

Roasted red & yellow kebabs

A feast for the eyes as well as the taste buds, this recipe is simple and colourful and a good way to tempt youngsters to eat vegetables. Tomatoes and peppers are great for a vitamin C boost and they are also full of beta-carotene.

Chinese five-spice powder or mixture of ground cumin and ground coriander 2 tsp
Olive oil 4 tsp
Cherry tomatoes 16, mixture of red and yellow

Red pepper 1, deseeded and cut into squares
Yellow pepper 1, deseeded and cut into squares

1 Preheat the oven to 200°C/400°F/Gas 6. In a small bowl, mix the five-spice powder or the cumin and coriander with the oil.

2 Thread the tomatoes and pieces of pepper onto four or eight bamboo skewers. Put them on a sturdy baking sheet and brush all over with the spicy marinade.

3 Cook in the oven for 8–10 minutes until the pepper has softened and the tomatoes are just about to split. Turn them once during cooking. Serve with oven-roasted chicken or fish with potatoes or rice or noodles.

Cook's tip

Make these kebabs into a posh starter by threading slices of smoked salmon among the tomatoes and peppers.

Preparation time **20 minutes**
Cooking time **10 minutes**
Calories per portion **54 Kcal**
Fat per portion **3g**
of which saturated **0.3g**
Serves **6**
Suitable for vegetarians

Mixed stir-fried mushrooms

Rather than the same old 'meat and two veg', why not try something different with your steak or roast chicken? This mushroom and vegetable dish is packed with flavour and tastes just delicious, as well as being really good for you.

Cook's tip

This stir-fry does not require any additional liquid as the mushrooms give off a lot of juice. If you prefer a thicker sauce, simply raise the heat to reduce the liquid slightly.

Shiitake or chestnut mushrooms 120g pack
Portabellini mushrooms 250g (9oz)
Corn oil 1 tbsp
Red pepper 1 large, deseeded, halved and cut into thin strips widthways

Spring onions 6, trimmed and cut into short lengths diagonally
Sweet chilli sauce 2 tbsp
Reduced salt soy sauce 1–2 tbsp
Bean sprouts 200g pack

1 Wash and thoroughly dry all the mushrooms. Depending on their size, thickly slice or leave whole.

2 Heat the oil in a large work or frying pan, then add the pepper strips and spring onions and stir-fry for 1–2 minutes, or until just beginning to soften.

3 Add all the prepared mushrooms and continue to stir-fry over a high heat for 3–4 minutes, or until the mushrooms just start to soften and give off their juices.

4 Add the sweet chilli sauce, soy sauce, and bean sprouts to the pan. Continue to stir-fry over a high heat until the sauce is hot and the bean sprouts are just beginning to soften. Serve the stir-fry immediately while hot.

Preparation time **10 minutes**
Cooking time **10 minutes**
Calories per portion **163 Kcal**
Fat per portion **2g**
of which saturated **1.1g**
Serves **4**
Suitable for vegetarians

Pesto pea mash

An unusual alternative to traditional mashed potatoes, this makes the ideal accompaniment to roast cod or other chunky white fish, topped with some roasted baby vine tomatoes. As it is made with quark, this pesto is lower in fat than standard pesto but it still tastes delicious.

Cook's tip

The low fat pesto paste is also great tossed into freshly cooked pasta.

Floury potatoes 350g (12oz), peeled and cut into small pieces
Frozen peas 350g (12oz)
Garlic 2 cloves

Basil leaves a small handful
Quark 110g (4oz)
Grated Parmesan-like cheese 2 tbsp

1 Place the potatoes in a large saucepan. Cover with water, bring to the boil and cook for 5 minutes. Add the frozen peas, bring back to the boil, cover and cook for a further 4–5 minutes until tender.

2 Drain the potatoes and peas and return to the saucepan. Mash well using a potato masher or fork, adding seasoning to taste. Cover and set aside.

3 Peel the garlic cloves and place in a small blender or spice grinder. Add the basil, quark and Parmesan. Season well and blend together to form a paste. Stir the pesto paste into the mashed vegetables and serve immediately.

Preparation time **10 minutes**
Cooking time **40 minutes**
Calories per portion **257 Kcal**
Fat per portion **8g**
of which saturated **4.3g**
Serves **4**
Suitable for vegetarians

Celeriac & potato mash

Celeriac, as its name implies, adds a subtle celery flavour to mashed potatoes. Steaming the potatoes and celeriac is preferable to boiling for this dish, as it prevents them from becoming too watery in texture. The addition of oats gives a scrumptious crunchy topping.

Cook's tip

This dish can be prepared 2–3 hours ahead of serving. Cover and store in the refrigerator until ready for reheating when required.

Potatoes 680g (1½lb), peeled and cut into quarters
Celeriac 350g (12oz), peeled, quartered and cut into thick slices
Half fat crème fraîche 4–5 tbsp
Chopped parsley 3 tbsp

Porridge oats 40g (1½oz)
Mature Cheddar, Double Gloucester or Red Leicester cheese 50–75g (2–3oz), coarsely grated
Mixed dried herbs ½ tsp, optional

1 Preheat the oven to 220°C/425°F/Gas 7. Steam the potatoes and celeriac together for 20–25 minutes, or until cooked. Or, boil gently together and then drain.

2 Put the cooked potatoes and celeriac into a bowl, add the crème fraîche and mash well together. Season with salt and pepper and then mix in the parsley.

3 Spoon the potato and celeriac into a shallow flameproof dish of approximately 1 litre (1¾ pints) capacity.

4 Mix together the oats, grated cheese and herbs and sprinkle evenly over the top of the potato and celeriac. Bake in the centre of the oven until the cheese has melted and the top is golden brown. Serve as a vegetable accompaniment to fish, meat or poultry.

Preparation time **5 minutes**
Cooking time **35 minutes**
Calories per portion **127 Kcal**
Fat per portion **4g**
of which saturated **0.4g**
Serves **4**
Suitable for vegetarians

Spanish potatoes

This recipe can be served with a selection of tapas or is great with grilled or roasted meat or fish. Tomatoes are full of vitamins A and C and lycopene, a powerful antioxidant. The healthiest way to eat them is cooked or processed as this helps with lycopene absorption.

Cook's tip

If you don't want to put the oven on, fry the potatoes in a large pan until browned all over. Use Spanish smoked paprika for a more authentic flavour

Small waxy new potatoes 500g (1lb 2oz)
Olive oil 4 tsp
Shallot or small onion 1, peeled and finely chopped
Garlic 1 clove, peeled and finely chopped

Red chilli 1 small, deseeded and finely chopped
Chopped tomatoes 227g can
Paprika ½ tsp

1 Preheat the oven to 200°C/400°F/Gas 6. Add the potatoes to a pan of boiling water and cook for 10–12 minutes until they are just tender. Drain and leave to dry in a colander.

2 Heat 3 teaspoons of the oil in a roasting tin in the oven, add the potatoes and cook them for 15–20 minutes until browned all over, turning a couple of times.

3 Meanwhile, make the sauce. Heat the rest of the oil in a small frying pan over a medium heat. Add the shallot or onion and fry for 5 minutes, then add the garlic and chilli and fry for another minute. Stir the chopped tomatoes and paprika into the mixture and cook for 5 minutes.

4 Sprinkle a little sea salt and black pepper, if required, over the potatoes, put them in a hot serving dish and serve the sauce separately or spoon the sauce over the top.

Preparation time **5 minutes**
Cooking time **10 minutes**
Calories per portion **111 Kcal**
Fat per portion **2g**
of which saturated **0g**
Serves **4**
Suitable for vegetarians

Tandoori potato wedges

With subtle Indian flavouring, these wedges make a healthy and interesting alternative to chips. They are especially good served with fish or as an alternative to rice with the vegetable curry on page 71.

Cook's tip

If you prefer more crispy wedges or do not have a microwave, bake the wedges in the oven at 190°C/375°F/Gas 5 for 35–45 minutes, until cooked.

Baking potatoes 2, scrubbed
Tandoori paste 2 tbsp

1 Cut each potato into 8 equal-sized wedges. Brush each wedge with the tandoori paste.

2 Place the wedges, skin-side down on a microwavable plate. Cover with film and pierce a hole in the centre. Cook in the microwave on full power for 6–8 minutes, until cooked through. Serve with low fat natural yogurt.

Preparation time **5 minutes plus standing**
Cooking time **45 minutes**
Calories per portion **87 Kcal**
Fat per portion **1g**
of which saturated **0g**
Serves **4**
Suitable for vegetarians

Garlic & herb roast potatoes

These tender, flavoursome roasties will add something special to a roast chicken dinner. As they are cooked with just a little oil and plenty of garlic and herbs, they are really tasty and certainly not inferior to traditional roast potatoes – they just contain less fat.

Cook's tip

These potatoes are also good served cold as a salad vegetable.

Baby new potatoes 450g (1lb), scrubbed
Garlic 1 bulb

Spray oil a few bursts
Rosemary 1 small bunch
Thyme 1 small bunch

1 Preheat the oven to 220°C/425°F/Gas 7. Place the potatoes on a baking tray lined with baking parchment. Break the garlic bulb into individual cloves and remove any loose papery white skin, but do not peel completely. Mix in with the potatoes.

2 Spray lightly with spray oil and sprinkle with sea salt and freshly ground black pepper to taste. Break up the herbs into small sprigs and sprinkle over the top. Roast in the oven for 40–45 minutes until golden, fragrant and cooked through. Stand for 10 minutes for the flavours to develop, discard any woody bits of herb, and then serve.

Preparation time **5 minutes**
Cooking time **30 minutes**
Calories per portion **237 Kcal**
Fat per portion **2g**
of which saturated **0.5g**
Serves **4**
Suitable for vegetarians + freezing

Cardamon rice

Brown rice takes longer to cook than white rice, but it's worth the wait as it has a lovely nutty flavour, and the higher fibre content means that it's healthier too. With the addition of cardamon, this rice works perfectly with curry and balti dishes.

Cook's tip

Instead of using water, you can use stock – for example, use chicken stock if it's to accompany a chicken dish, or fish stock if it's to accompany a fish recipe.

Brown rice 250g (9oz)
Water 600ml (1 pint)
Onion 1, peeled and chopped
Cardamon pods 8, split open
Coriander sprig, to garnish

1 Rinse the rice and drain it well. Tip into a saucepan and add the water, onion and cardamon. Bring to the boil, then cover the pan with a tightly fitting lid and simmer gently for 25–30 minutes until the rice is almost tender.

2 Remove the lid from the pan and simmer the rice until the water has all been absorbed and the rice is tender. Fluff the rice through with a fork and season to taste and garnish with corianger leaves before serving with the curry of your choice.

Delicious
DESSERTS

Preparation time **20 minutes**
Cooking time **15–20 minutes**
Calories per portion **98 Kcal**
Fat per portion **2g**
of which saturated **0.2g**
Serves **6**
Suitable for vegetarians + freezing

Peaches cooked in rosé wine

Originally from China, peaches are succulent fruit that have long been praised in literature. In this recipe, they are lightly poached in rosé wine for a velvety texture and slightly alcoholic flavour. Peaches are a good source of vitamin A, which is essential for healthy skin.

Cook's tip

If serving the peaches cold, they can be prepared and cooked the day before.

Firm but ripe peaches 6 large
Cinnamon stick 5cm (2in) piece, halved
Rosé wine 500ml (18fl oz)
Caster sugar 25g (1oz)

Orange 1 large, very finely pared rind and juice
Half fat crème fraîche or quark or low fat natural yogurt to serve
Sliced pistachio nuts for sprinkling

1 Cut the peaches in half and carefully remove the stones. Place the peach halves in a single layer in a large, shallow saucepan. Add the cinnamon stick pieces, wine, sugar, orange rind and juice.

2 Place the saucepan over a moderate heat and bring the wine up to the boil. Reduce the heat, cover the pan with a tightly fitting lid and gently cook the peaches for 5–10 minutes (depending on their size), until they are only just softened when tested with the tip of a knife.

3 When the peaches are cooked, remove the pan from the heat. Using a large slotted spoon, remove the peaches from the wine and transfer them into a large heatproof serving dish.

4 Return the saucepan to the heat, bring the wine back up to the boil and then boil gently until the wine is reduced by about two-thirds or until slightly syrupy.

5 Pour the wine over the peaches and allow them to cool. When cold, cover and refrigerate until well chilled. Serve with crème fraîche, quark or yogurt and sprinkled with pistachio nuts. If preferred, the peaches may also be served hot.

Preparation time **5 minutes**
Cooking time **10 minutes**
Calories per portion **79 Kcal**
Fat per portion **0g**
of which saturated **0g**
Serves **4**
Suitable for vegetarians + freezing

Mulled grapes

It is believed that one portion of grapes a day can help protect your heart and one glass of red wine a day can reduce the risk of heart disease. Flavonoids in red wine and grapes help oxidise the bad cholesterol, so this is a heart-friendly dessert.

Cook's tip

Warn people that the grapes are hot!

Sweet fruity red wine 150ml (¼ pint)
Light muscovado sugar 1 tbsp
Root ginger 2cm (¾in) piece, peeled and halved

Whole cloves 4
Red and green grapes 350g (12oz) mixed

1 Pour the wine into a small pan with 150ml (¼ pint) water and the sugar. Stud the ginger pieces with the cloves and add them to the pan. Heat gently, stirring until the sugar dissolves.

2 Add the grapes and simmer for 3–5 minutes. Turn off the heat. Remove the ginger pieces. Spoon the grapes into warm glasses and top up with the mulled wine.

Preparation time **10 minutes**
Cooking time **10 minutes**
Calories per kebab **60 Kcal**
Fat per kebab **0g**
of which saturated **0g**
Makes **8 kebabs**
Suitable for vegetarians

Honeyed fruit kebabs

These kebabs are perfect for summer entertaining as you can also cook them on a barbecue. The honey is thought to alleviate hay fever and so this may help some guests, particularly if you are in the garden! The kebabs look really attractive and taste even better.

Honey 2 tbsp
Lime 1, zest only
Vanilla extract few drops
Pineapple ½, peeled (optional), cored and cubed

Mango 1, peeled, stoned and cubed
Raspberries 110g (4oz)
Icing sugar 1–2 tbsp

1 Preheat the grill to a medium setting. Mix together the honey, lime zest and vanilla extract as a glaze for the fruit. Stir the mango and pineapple into the glaze until evenly coated.

2 Thread the pineapple and mango pieces onto eight wooden skewers. Brush with any remaining honey mixture. Cook the skewers under the grill for 5–7 minutes, turning them occasionally until the fruit starts to turn golden at the edges.

3 Mash the raspberries and stir in the icing sugar to taste. Serve the hot kebabs with some of the raspberry sauce in a small dish as a dip or drizzled over them.

Cook's tip

If you're using wooden skewers, soak them in water for 5–10 minutes before threading the fruit onto them and they will then be less likely to burn.

Preparation time **10 minutes**

Cooking time **10 minutes**

Calories per portion **183 Kcal**

Fat per portion **11g**

of which saturated **6.5g**

Serves **4**

Suitable for vegetarians

Roast figs with ginger thins

Fresh figs have a short season in late summer so do take advantage of them as they are high in fibre and potassium. Dried figs are ideal for a snack but they contain more calories than fresh, although on the plus side they have a higher concentration of minerals.

Cook's tip

The biscuits will keep in an airtight tin for a few days or freeze in a rigid container for up to 3 months. Thaw at room temperature for an hour.

Butter 40g (1½oz) for the thins, plus 15g (½oz) for the figs

Egg 1, white only

Caster sugar 25g (1oz)

Plain flour 25g (1oz)

Ground ginger ½ tsp

Figs 4, halved

Soft light brown sugar 1 tsp

Marsala, Madeira or ginger wine 2 tbsp

1 To make the ginger thins, preheat the oven to 200°C/400°F/Gas 6. Lightly grease two baking sheets. Melt 40g (1½oz) of the butter.

2 Lightly whisk the egg white with a fork to break it up, then add the caster sugar and whisk to combine. Sift the flour and ginger into the sugar and egg white and then fold them in together with the melted butter. Mix lightly.

3 Put teaspoonfuls of the mixture onto the baking sheets and spread out to about 7.5cm (3in). Make two batches each of 6 or 7 biscuits. Bake each batch for 5 minutes until pale golden. Leave a few seconds to firm, then remove with a palette knife and drape over a rolling pin to cool, curl and crisp.

4 Heat the rest of the butter in a pan and fry the figs, cut-side down for 2 minutes, until browned. Turn over the figs, stir in the brown sugar and then the wine and cook for another 1–2 minutes until syrupy.

5 Serve the figs on plates with the sauce drizzled over them and one or two ginger thins per person.

Preparation time **20 minutes**
Cooking time **15 minutes**
Calories per portion **177 Kcal**
Fat per portion **1g**
of which saturated **0g**
Serves **4**
Suitable for vegetarians

Melon balls with caramel

Melons are a good source of vitamins A and C and so they are crucial in caring for the skin and eyes as well as looking after the immune system. They are very attractive fruits, particularly when cut into balls, as in this dish.

Cook's tip

This dessert can be made with other combinations of fresh fruits, such as strawberries with cherries and/or sliced peaches or segmented oranges.

Caster sugar 75g (3oz)
Canteloupe melon 1 large
Galia melon 1 large

Grand Marnier or other orange liqueur, kirsch or brandy 3 tbsp
Orange slices, strawberries, cherries to decorate

1 Line a plate, baking tray or sponge sandwich tin with non-stick paper or non-stick foil. Half-fill a small saucepan with water and bring to the boil.

2 Put the sugar into another small saucepan, add 2 tablespoons of cold water and then stir continuously over a moderate heat until every granule of the sugar is dissolved – brushing the sides of the pan down frequently with the boiling water (to prevent the syrup forming crystals).

3 When every granule of sugar is dissolved, bring the syrup to the boil and boil until it turns into a light, golden caramel colour. Immediately pour the caramel onto the prepared tray and leave it to set hard.

4 To prepare the melons, cut each in half and remove the seeds. Using a melon-baller, scoop the melon flesh into a bowl (to catch the juice). Add the Grand Marnier, or other liqueur, and gently mix together.

5 When the caramel is hard, cover it with non-stick baking paper and use a heavy kitchen weight or the end of a rolling pin to break and crush the caramel into small pieces.

6 Layer the melon balls (including the juice) and crushed caramel alternately in attractive serving glasses, ending with a layer of caramel. Reserve some caramel to decorate. Decorate and serve immediately.

Preparation time **10 minutes**
Calories per sundae **220 Kcal**
Fat per sundae **10g**
of which saturated **5.8g**
Makes **4 sundaes**
Suitable for vegetarians

Fruity Italian sundaes

Berries really are super-fruits, rich in antioxidants that help protect against cancer. They also have anti-viral and anti-bacterial properties and help to look after the eyes. The custard and crème fraîche in these desserts provide lashings of calcium, too.

Amaretti biscotti 60g (2½oz), broken into small pieces
Strawberries 110g (4oz), hulled and sliced

Blueberries 110g (4oz)
Raspberries 110g (4oz)
Low fat custard 300g (11oz)
Half fat crème fraîche 200ml (7fl oz)

1 Place half of the amaretti biscuits in the bottom of four sundae or wine glasses.

2 Reserving a few strawberry slices, 8 blueberries and 4 raspberries for decoration, divide the strawberries between the glasses. Add a quarter of the blueberries to each glass and then top with the raspberries, equally divided. Sprinkle most of the remaining biscotti over the raspberries.

3 Mix together the custard and crème fraîche and pour the mixture over the fruit and amaretti. Chill until required and then decorate with the remaining strawberry slices, blueberries, raspberries and biscotti before serving.

Cook's tip

In place of the strawberries, blueberries and raspberries, peel, core and chop some dessert apples and add a few raisins. Cook together in a lidded saucepan, over a low heat until the apples have softened.

Preparation time **10 minutes**
Cooking time **10 minutes**
Calories per portion **58 Kcal**
Fat per portion **0.4g**
of which saturated **0.1g**
Serves **4**
Suitable for vegetarians

Gooseberry fool

This is quick to make during the summer months when fresh gooseberries are available. Native to the UK, gooseberries are simply delicious stewed with a little sugar, but are virtually unknown in other parts of the world. The French don't even have a name for them!

Cook's tip

Although this dessert needs to be eaten shortly after making, or the whisked egg whites will collapse, the gooseberry and ginger purée may be cooked a day or two in advance and kept in the fridge.

Gooseberries 250g (9oz), topped and tailed
Water 3–4 tbsp
Root ginger 5mm (¼in) piece, peeled and grated

Honey 3 tbsp
Low fat natural yogurt 75g (3oz)
Egg 1, white only

1 Tip the gooseberries into a saucepan and add the water, ginger and 2 tablespoons of honey. Place the pan over a medium heat and bring to a simmer. Reduce the heat and let the fruit simmer gently for 5–8 minutes, or until the gooseberries mash to a pulp. Leave the purée to cool then fold the yogurt into the gooseberry purée.

2 Whisk the egg white until stiff and fold it into the purée. Spoon into serving dishes and serve immediately with the remaining honey drizzled on top.

Preparation time **20 minutes**
Cooking time **10 minutes plus freezing time**
Calories per portion **165 Kcal**
Fat per portion **1g**
of which saturated **0.2g**
Serves **4**
Suitable for vegetarians + freezing

Lime & kiwi sorbet

Kiwis have the highest vitamin C concentration of any fruit so they are a great force against age-related diseases. They are also a rich source of antioxidants, vitamins E and K and magnesium (for a healthy heart). This tangy sorbet makes the perfect summer pudding.

Cook's tip

To ring the changes, use elderflower or lemon grass and lime cordial if you like.

Lime cordial 100ml (3½fl oz)
Caster sugar 75g (3oz)

Kiwi fruits 6
Low fat natural yogurt 150g (5oz)

1 In a small, heavy-based saucepan, mix the lime cordial with 200ml (7fl oz) water and the sugar. Bring to the boil, then simmer for 2 minutes to dissolve the sugar. Bring back to the boil and continue to boil for 5 minutes. Transfer to a bowl and leave to cool.

2 Halve the kiwi fruit and scoop out the flesh with a teaspoon into a food processor. Purée the fruit then add the lime syrup and yogurt and whiz again.

3 Pour into a plastic container and freeze for about 3 hours until slushy. Put back into the processor and whiz for one more time. Spoon back into the freezer container and leave it to freeze. Alternatively, put the mixture in an ice-cream maker and follow the manufacturer's instructions.

4 Place spoonfuls of sorbet – it will be not be frozen too firm – in individual glasses and serve.

Preparation time **10 minutes**
Freezing time **6 hours but less with**
an ice-cream maker
Calories per portion **146 Kcal**
Fat per portion **2g**
of which saturated **0.9g**
Serves **8**
Suitable for vegetarians + freezing

Cherry yogurt ice

When cherries are plentiful, make a batch of this creamy low fat ice cream for a refreshing treat. You can also make it with raspberries, strawberries or blueberries. Fruit are always best eaten when they are in season, so choose whatever is in abundance.

Low fat vanilla bio live yogurt
2 x 500g tubs
Semi-skimmed milk 6 tbsp

Caster sugar 25g (1oz)
Cherries 225g (8oz), halved and stoned

1 Pour one tub of yogurt into a large plastic container. Whisk in the milk and sugar and then whisk in the other pot of yogurt. Put the lid on and freeze for 3 hours until almost solid.

2 Break up the icy mixture and whisk well until almost smooth. Stir in the halved cherries and put the mixture back in the freezer for another 3 hours until firm. Take the ice cream out of the freezer 10 minutes before serving.

Cook's tip

If you have an ice-cream maker, put the yogurt mixture in and follow the manufacturer's instructions, adding the cherries towards the end of the process.

Preparation time **10 minutes**
Cooking time **5 minutes**
Calories per brulée **157 Kcal**
Fat per brulée **1g**
of which saturated **0.5g**
Makes **4 brulées**
Suitable for vegetarians

Raspberry Turkish delight brulées

The exotic flavour of rose water blends deliciously with raspberries. Originally cultivated in Greece, raspberries are a good source of magnesium, vitamin C and potassium. For a change, try small halved strawberries or even cubes of orange-fleshed melon.

Raspberries 350g (12oz), thawed if frozen
Natural essence of rose water 4 tsp

Low fat natural yogurt 300g (11oz)
Pink Turkish delight 50g (2oz)
Demerara sugar 4 tbsp

1 Divide the raspberries between four large ramekin dishes. Sprinkle 1 teaspoon rose water over each dish. Pour the yogurt into a bowl, then cut the Turkish delight into small pieces and mix into the yogurt. Spoon over the raspberries to cover.

2 Preheat the grill to a hot setting. Arrange the ramekins in the grill tray, and sprinkle each with 1 tablespoon sugar. Grill for 3–4 minutes, until the sugar melts and caramelises. Stand for 1 minute to allow the sugar to set before serving.

Cook's tip

If you have more time, place the fruit in a shallow bowl and sprinkle over the rose water. Cover and stand for 30 minutes to allow the flavours to infuse.

Preparation time **15 minutes plus
cooling and setting**
Calories per jelly **128 Kcal**
Fat per jelly **5g**
of which saturated **2.3g**
Makes **4 jellies**

Chocolate orange jellies

All the family will love these little chocolatey pots. They make a real treat, and are surprisingly low in fat. They are also a sneaky way of encouraging children to get some of their calcium and boost their vitamin C intake.

Cook's tip

If you prefer a tangier flavour, replace the fromage frais with low fat natural yogurt or quark.

Cocoa powder 25g (1oz)
Sugar-free orange jelly crystals 1 sachet
Caster sugar 2 tbsp
Orange juice of 1 large

Half fat crème fraîche 4 tsp, to decorate
Peeled orange segments 4
Plain chocolate 25g (1oz), grated

1 Put the cocoa and orange jelly crystals into a jug and gradually mix in 150ml (¼ pint) boiling water until smooth. Stir in the sugar until it has dissolved, then mix in the orange juice.

2 Top up with cold water to make 600ml (1 pint) and pour into four glasses. Chill for at least 2 hours until set.

3 To decorate, add a spoonful of crème fraîche and an orange segment to the top of each dessert. Sprinkle with a little grated chocolate.

Preparation time **5 minutes**
Cooking time **15 minutes**
Calories per portion **291 Kcal**
Fat per portion **5g**
of which saturated **1.6g**
Serves **2**
Suitable for vegetarians

Pain perdu with caramelised plums

The translation of *pain perdu* is 'lost bread', which comes from the fact that it's a way of using older bread that may otherwise be thrown away. The plums provide fibre and vitamin C, and have a scrumptiously sweet taste that works wonderfully with the 'eggy' bread.

Cook's tip

Use dessert apples instead of plums. Core the apples and slice them, then cook in the same way as the plums.

Egg 1
Semi-skimmed milk 6 tbsp
Wholemeal bread 2 slices
Spray oil 2 bursts

Caster sugar 4 tbsp
Water 3 tbsp
Plums 3, halved and stoned

1 Lightly beat together the egg and milk in a shallow dish that is just slightly larger then the slices of bread. Soak each slice of bread on each side in the eggy mixture.

2 Heat a non-stick frying pan over a medium heat. Spray the base of the pan with the olive oil spray and add the bread to the pan. Cook the bread for 2–3 minutes on each side, until it's a light golden colour. Remove the bread from the pan and keep it warm while cooking the plums.

3 Wipe out the frying pan with a piece of kitchen paper. Place the pan over the heat and sprinkle over a thin layer of sugar. Keep the pan over a low heat until the sugar caramelises then sprinkle over a little more sugar and let that caramelise. Repeat in this way until all the sugar has caramelised. Add the water to the pan and leave it to melt into the caramel.

4 Add the plums to the caramel in the pan, placing them cut-side down. Cook for 2–3 minutes, then turn them over and cook for a further 1–2 minutes, or until the plums are tender.

5 Arrange 6 plum halves on each slice of eggy bread and spoon over the juices in the pan and serve immediately with low fat natural Greek yogurt.

Preparation time **45 minutes plus cooling time and overnight chilling**
Cooking time **20 minutes**
Calories per pudding **273 Kcal**
Fat per pudding **1g**
of which saturated **0.2g**
Makes **6 puddings**
Suitable for vegetarians + freezing

Tropical summer puddings

These little puddings look very impressive when served to family or friends. This is a very low fat dessert that provides beta-carotene and a variety of vitamins and counts as two of the recommended five-a-day portions of fruit and vegetables.

Cooking apples 2 large
Caster sugar 75g (3oz)
Lemon juice 1 tbsp
Trifle sponge cakes 12
Pineapple 175g (6oz) prepared weight

Mango 1 large, peeled, stoned and chopped
Raspberries 250g (9oz)
Mint leaves to decorate
Icing sugar for sifting, optional

1 Peel, core and slice the apples. Put into a saucepan, add 2 tablespoons of water and the caster sugar and lemon juice. Cover the saucepan with a tightly fitting lid and cook the apple over a moderate heat for 15–20 minutes, or until cooked and fluffy in texture. When the apple is cooked, pour it into a nylon or stainless steel sieve, placed over a bowl, to drain and cool until cold.

2 Cut each trifle sponge cake into three thin slices horizontally. Using a 1.5cm (1in) plain round cutter, stamp out six rounds from 3–4 of the sponge slices, reserving the trimmings. Place a sponge round in the bottom of each cup or mould. Then, trimming the sponge slices to fit, line the sides, allowing a little of the sponge to protrude above the rim. Again, reserve the trimmings.

3 Put the pineapple and mango into a mixing bowl, add the drained apple and mix together. Then gently fold in the raspberries.

4 Spoon the fruit into the lined cups or moulds, reserving some pieces for decorating. Cover the tops with the remaining pieces of sponge cake (cutting to fit where necessary).

5 Securely cover the tops of the puddings with cling film, and then place them on a tray. Next, place something heavy on top of each pudding, e.g. kitchen weights or canned foods, to weight down the mixture. Chill the puddings overnight.

6 When ready to serve, remove the weights and cling film. Place a serving plate on top of the cups or moulds, and then invert. Remove the cups or moulds from the puddings. Decorate with the reserved fruit and mint leaves. Sift lightly with icing sugar, if using, and serve with fromage frais or quark.

Preparation time **40 minutes**
Cooking time **10–12 minutes**
Calories per portion **175 Kcal**
Fat per portion **4g**
of which saturated **0.9g**
Serves **6**
Suitable for vegetarians + freezing

Raspberry sponge flan

Quick and easy to make, this fatless sponge flan is filled with quark and raspberries and a high fruit content spread that has no added sugar. Think of it as a healthy indulgence, perfect to follow a family Sunday lunch.

Cook's tip

The flan may also be made with a mixture of raspberries and sliced strawberries or all strawberries, if preferred.

Eggs 3 large
Caster sugar 75g (3oz)
Vanilla extract ½ tsp
Plain flour 75g (3oz)
Quark 75g (3oz)

Apricot high fruit content spread (no added sugar) 2 tbsp
Raspberries 250g (9oz)
Icing sugar for sifting
Mint leaves to decorate

1 To make the sponge flan case, preheat the oven to 180°C/350°F/Gas 4. Lightly grease and flour a 25cm (10in) sponge flan tin.

2 Break the eggs into a large mixing bowl, add the caster sugar and vanilla extract and then whisk together (preferably with a hand-held electric mixer) for approximately 10 minutes, until the mixture becomes very thick and creamy, and light in colour.

3 Gently sift the flour into the bowl and then carefully fold the flour into the egg mixture using a large metal spoon. Pour the mixture into the prepared flan tin, spread it evenly across the base and bake for 10–12 minutes, or until well risen, feels springy to the touch and has slightly shrunk away from the sides of the tin.

4 Allow the flan case to cool in the tin for 5–10 minutes, then carefully turn it out onto a wire rack to cool completely. Transfer it onto a serving plate.

5 Put the quark and fruit spread into a bowl and gently blend together with a wire whisk or fork.

6 Spread the apricot mixture over the bottom of the flan case, and then arrange the raspberries in circles on top and scatter over mint leaves. Sift icing sugar over the top, then cover and keep refrigerated until ready to serve.

Preparation time **10 minutes**
Cooking time **5 minutes**
Calories per pudiing **125 Kcal**
Fat per pudding **1g**
of which saturated **0g**
Makes **6 rice puddings**
Suitable for vegetarians

Pear & apricot rice pudding

A comforting fruit pudding that's super speedy to make and cook. It uses canned fruit and rice for convenience, so is perfect for when you need a sweet treat mid-week and don't have lots of spare time. The crispy topping gives the pudding added texture.

Cook's tip

The fruit under the rice only heats up slightly during cooking, so if you prefer, heat the fruit in its canning juices for 2–3 minutes until hot but not boiling, and then drain and spoon into the dishes. Top and grill immediately.

Pear halves in natural juice 411g can
Apricot halves in natural juice 411g can
Low fat rice pudding 425g can

Demerara sugar 3 tbsp
Fresh wholemeal breadcrumbs 3 tbsp
Ground nutmeg ¼ tsp

1 Drain the pear and apricot halves, and cut into small pieces. Place in the bottom of six large ramekin dishes or small ovenproof gratin dishes.

2 Spoon the rice pudding evenly over the top of the fruit, making sure it is completely covered. Mix together the sugar, breadcrumbs and nutmeg and sprinkle over the top of the rice.

3 Preheat the grill to hot. Place the dishes in the grill tray and grill for 3–4 minutes until crisp, golden and bubbling – the sugar will start to melt and caramelise. Stand for 1 minute to allow the sugar to set before serving.

Preparation time **10 minutes**
Cooking time **30 minutes**
Calories per portion **185 Kcal**
Fat per portion **1g**
of which saturated **0.2g**
Serves **4**
Suitable for vegetarians + freezing

Apple & plum crumble

Rather than make a traditional crumble mixture using flour, here oats are used as a topping. Oats are an excellent source of soluble fibre, which helps to reduce blood cholesterol levels, and as the energy from them is released slowly, you'll feel full for longer.

Cooking apples 450g (1lb), peeled, cored and sliced
Plums 450g (1lb), stoned and quartered
Ground cinnamon 1 tsp

Cornflour 1 tbsp
Demerara sugar 3 tbsp
Jumbo oats 3 tbsp
Spray oil 2–3 bursts

1 Preheat the oven to 190°C/375°F/Gas 5. Mix together the apple slices, plums, cinnamon, cornflour and 2 tablespoons of the demerara sugar. Tip the mixture into an ovenproof dish. Drizzle with 6 tablespoons of water.

2 Sprinkle the oats over the top and then the sprinkle with the remaining sugar. Spray 2–3 bursts of oil over the top of the oats. Bake in the centre of the oven for 20–30 minutes or until the topping is a light golden colour and the apples feel tender when pierced with a skewer. Serve with low fat natural yogurt.

Cook's tip

For a crunchier topping, use jumbo rolled oats or 'traditional'-style oats, which are larger than normal rolled oats.

Index

Previous books

Dairy Cookbooks are widely recognised as some of the most reliable recipe books ever written. With over 30 million copies sold, almost every household will have used a Dairy Cookbook at some point. The first book – *The Dairy Book of Home Cookery* – was published in 1968 and has been revised and reprinted several times due to its unprecedented popularity. In recent years, four new cookbooks have been published – *The New Dairy Cookbook*, the *Quick & Easy Dairy Cookbook*, the *Year Round Dairy Cookbook* and *Around Britain Dairy Cookbook*.

For pricing and ordering details please ring:

01536 762922

There is more information on our website:

www.dairydiary.co.uk

The Dairy Book of Home Cookery (416 pages) was last published in 1992, and contains hundreds of recipes, from how to make the perfect cheese sauce to creating an impressive soufflé.

The New Dairy Cookbook (192 pages) was published in 2001 and features 150 delicious new recipes for all occasions.

Quick & Easy Dairy Cookbook (192 pages) was published in 2003 and has 130 tasty recipes, which can be prepared in less than 30 minutes.

Year Round Dairy Cookbook (192 pages), published in 2005 and features 130 seasonal recipes to give the taste buds a treat the whole year round.

Around Britain Dairy Cookbook (192 pages) was published in 2006 and contains favourite regional recipes as well as new ones with a contemporary twist.

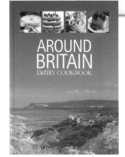